JONES ONIGBINDE

Great MOTHER HEART

THE FASCINATING STORY OF RESILIENCE, INSPIRATION & ENDURING LOVE OF A MOTHER

JONES ONIGBINDE

MOTHER HEART
Great

THE FACINATING STORY OF
RESILIENCE, INSPIRATION
& ENDURING LOVE OF A MOTHER

WORKBOOK PRESS LLC
187 E Warm Springs Rd,
Suite B285, Las Vegas, NV 89119, USA

Website: https://workbookpress.com/
Hotline: 1-888-818-4856
Email: admin@workbookpress.com

Ordering Information:
Quantity sales. Special discounts are available on quantity purchases by corporations, associations, and others. For details, contact the publisher at the address above.

Library of Congress Control Number:

ISBN-13:   978-1-961845-29-9 (Paperback Version)
                978-1-961845-30-5 (Digital Version)

REV. DATE: 08/02/2023

Dedication

This book is dedicated to my beloved wife, Tanya, who exemplifies the best in motherhood. Her tireless efforts in raising our children to love Christ and the Kingdom are a constant reminder of my mother's influence in my life. I'm so glad my wife is keeping my mother's legacies alive in our home.

This book is also dedicated to my beloved daughter, Evangelina. Her tender heart and love for Christ assure me that my mother's legacy of love, kindness, and inspiration will be carried on far into the future.

Acknowledgement

Without the support and encouragement of my family and friends, this book would not have materialized.

First, thanks go to my beloved wife Tanya, who, through her dedication to our home, gave me the anchor and focus I needed for this project. I would also like to thank our children, Evangelina, Nathan, and Nehemiah, you all bring profound joy to our hearts every day.

I'm also blessed with friends who helped and encouraged me along the way. They include, Steve Jamam, Olumide Oteniya, Frederick Omojola, Idowu Odebiyi, Elias Enoaku, and a host of others who I cannot mention. Special thanks go to Stu Wigle, a friend that stuck by me more than a brother. It's only the Divine that can bring a black man from a back street in Africa to join him in friendship with a white man in the northern city of Fort MacMurray. Thank you, Stu, for all your help and steady friendship throughout all these years.

Thank you to my sister, Funmilola Adeyemo, and Grandma, Zoila Travis, for all your support and encouragement.

About the Author

J ones ONIGBINDE has been a Physical Therapist since 1998, after graduating with a Bachelor of Medical Rehabilitation degree from Obafemi Awolowo University, Ile-Ife, Nigeria. He is the founder and the CEO of Stargate Physical Therapy Inc., a multidisciplinary medical rehabilitation facility in Calgary, Alberta. He also founded Great Mother Heart Inc., an organization dedicated to the promotion of issues affecting the mother and child. He is married to Tanya Onigbinde, with whom he has three children: Evangelina, Nathan and Nehemiah.

Preface

When we talk about love, there is no love as powerful, as liberating, and as pure as that of a mother. From the day we are born to the day one of us leaves the world forever, the mother remains, dedicated to shower us with affection and care that knows no bounds. Even when we're grown up and we don't have much time to visit them, a mother makes sure our favorite apple pie is hot out of the oven and ready, waiting for us when we do. If that is not unconditional love, then what is?

Throughout my life, my mother has been my biggest inspiration. She has been my most prominent teacher, my strongest support system, and my best role model. This book is a tribute to her life and legacy. It is also, I hope, an inspiration for mothers struggling to strike a balance in their lives to bring up their children in the most effective manner. This book is the story of my life - it's the story of my mother.

Table of Contents

CHAPTER 1

From Birth to Childhood

My mother dreamed for me even before I could dream of my own success - she was the one who trusted in me. Her trust was in my robust skills and talent, this led me to the position which I hold today! It was her love that made everything possible and enabled me to achieve everything I have. Raising me was a challenge and struggle for her, but she didn't ever make me feel it. Instead, she just kept motivating me. I will never forget that day when, with an agonized facial expression - loud enough to express her anxiety - she gripped me firmly by the hand with her rough fingertips and warned me about not going too close to the river bank. Being a child, I could not understand the consequences - the river was deep, and the water roared quickly passed us.

I saw fear in her dark eyes, she urged me to use my feet, as tears rolled down her cheeks. My unresponsiveness alarmed her even more, so she used both her hands and tugged me out of the water. She ended up slipping in the mud and her face got covered in it. I lay near a tree, I took some water in my tiny palms from a pot nearby and cleaned her face with it. She smiled at me, then she hugged me so tight that I could not speak. I knew then that she never wanted me to get hurt, she wanted something else for me - she had bright dreams for me.

She wanted me to achieve the status that very few people in our village had ever managed - she wanted me to succeed and create a name for myself. Her undying efforts, her tireless sacrifices, all for my sake. She was my wall-like support, my protector and my sustainer. Her vision for me and her ambition to help me succeed, was her primary concern. My success was of upmost importance to her and nothing in life made her happier than to work toward this, so that one day, together, we would achieve her goal. She wanted her youngest son to become the biggest man.

For a woman like her, there was never an easy day. Her trust in my skills, and her belief in my talents and intellect led me to be in a position which I had not even dreamed of when I was young. It was her determination and die-hard efforts that pulled us through the difficult times. She loved me unconditionally. She kept me away from the miseries which she had to encounter every day of her life, living in that village. She kept motivating me; she kept telling me that I could do it.

My childhood had its own nightmares and troubles, but my mother became an umbrella and shielded me during the storms. It was her body that was soaked in all the rain and was battered by all the harsh winds and thunders.

I cannot forget the times I spent in the old village in Nigeria, West Africa, where resources were so few. Water was scarce, and we had no electricity or gas, but none of these deficiencies were large enough to conquer my mother's dreams. She had named me Obalolu, meaning *"the Lord is the King."* (My grandpa named me Jones, the welsh variant of John.) I never asked her why she chose Obalolu, but now I understand - she counted me as a blessing.

My mother once told me, "*I remember the occasion vividly. You were about to come into this world. It was a Sunday morning and, on the far east side of the village, I could hear the church bells ringing for the morning prayer. As I struggled with the labor pain, the bell was calling the people to church, and you came into this world as the they rang tirelessly. I can still listen to them, if I close my eyes. It was around 9 a.m. to 10 a.m. on July 9th, 1972.*"

My birth meant so much to her. She used to tell me that she could never forget that blessed day when she heard the bells, and she believed that God had a purpose behind my coming into this world, as I was not an ordinary child, I was born with a purpose.

At that moment, she had decided that '*this child of mine will succeed. He will grow up to do great things.*' She dreamed of me going to university; she dreamed of me becoming a role model for the whole community. It is fair to say that she did not dream of anything else. For me, my existence was her dream and she infused those dreams and goals into my soul. She would remind me of my purpose whenever we were talking; whenever we were on the farm; whenever we went to the river; and especially whenever we went to the church.

The days were hot and having a roof over our heads was a great blessing. Our house or, more accurately, our hut or shack, was very small for the size of the family that we had. We were six siblings, and I had the privilege of being the youngest. My father had two wives (both living together), and we also had our grandfather living under the same roof as well. I can still vividly remember that the house was dilapidated. It was a place where I could not call my friends and, if a visitor came, we did not have any space for them. This was the case for the families in more than half of our village; it was considered the norm, so the people didn't even contemplate the need to strive for better lives.

My mother though, she had dreams. She wanted me to become someone important in our village. The villagers would taunt me, calling me the 'city guy', but for my mother, this would be an honored title.

My childhood home - Back view.
To give you a perspective of where I grew up -
a dilapidated house has been like this for almost 30 yrs.

Like many of the houses in the village, ours was built from mud and pieces of brick. It was only still standing because the walls were thick - this was the only way to fight the harsh winds and hot sun. Our roof was made from scraps of tin and dried leaves. While many of the houses had proper roofs, we could not afford one.

When I was only four years old, my father passed away, he had left no fortune or property to us, we were on our own, and none of my siblings were earning a living. Our father had left us a year earlier before his death, as he had grown very sick. Our village did not have the facilities to support his continuously deteriorating health, so he was sent to the big city to our uncle. His brother took care of him until the day he passed away.

He was never a bad person, but he was passive, and he allowed grandpa to dictate what happened in our own nuclear family - he acceded to everything grandpa said. It was grandpa's idea that my siblings remained on the family farm - my father agreed to this. It is safe to say that my father wasn't his own man. His father was in control for the most part, and this was my father's own fault.

After my father was buried and his last rights were read, everyone went back to their lives, but my mother was faced with some very hard decisions about her life. She was young enough to get married again - her husband was not alive, and remarrying could've brought her some support with six children to feed. However, she was aware of the problems she would be faced with if she remarried - the trouble of coping with the needs of a new husband and taking care of her six children. She was a mother first - her needs came second to anything that was in favor of her children and she chose them. After my father's death, my mother never remarried.

After his death, things were no easier. My mother had entered her widowhood; I cannot explain the feelings she might have had. At least before this, she had someone to look to for money and other basic needs. Our lives changed completely - it was as if we were caught in the middle of a turbulent storm. My siblings took his death as an opportunity to move on with their personal lives and pursue their dreams, as they were bound to staying in the village when he was alive. Most of them went to the city to seek out opportunities and to build a livelihood.

These sudden changes in our lives felt like an avalanche on my mother's shoulder. I was too young to understand these circumstances and the consequences of my siblings' actions back then, but now I know how hard it must have been for her.

After all the transitions, my mother and I were left alone in the house. My siblings had chosen different paths, they had all wanted to go to school and study at college, as they too wanted to make a better life for themselves - a better life than the one our father had given us - and to live in a better place. They never liked the farm and so some of my siblings went to the big cities, some to live with my uncles and aunties, while others continued to pursue their education.

My mother had a strong yet heavy heart: she let each of them go, wanting them to live their lives as they wished, but she was sad about their departure, and often cried for them. I still don't know how my mother thought so wisely, or is it in every mother's heart to love her cubs unconditionally - as a lioness takes care of her young ones, carrying them to safety, feeding them and saving them from intruders?

My siblings did not forget us completely; we hoped that they would provide for us from working in the city. As it was believed in the village, the big city meant big money. But this proved to be false. Whenever they came to visit us, my mother's face would light up. She would smile at them, hug them for very long minutes, shed some tears and ask them how they were, how the city was, where they lived, and where they worked. She wanted to know everything about them. But often, they only came to ask us for financial help.

She never said no. She worked on the farm alone. I was with her and helped as much as I could, but when it was too hot, she would sit me under a shade, and carry on working. She worked all day on the farm, she had to do all this to provide for us and to feed us, because we were all she had. The farm that was left for us was soon taken away by the extended family, leaving my mother to work on other people's farms and earn a living working all day, every day.

My mother could have said that the world wasn't fair, and she would have been right, for all I know. She could have blamed the same God, to whom she prayed daily, for my father's death when I was only four. She could have blamed my father, the system, the community or our country for our circumstances and abject poverty. She could have bemoaned her fate as a widowed mother of six children. But she did none of these. She did what a mother could have done best, she persevered. She stood her ground. The tides were against her, but she sailed anyway.

When I reached the age of six, she had decided to send me to primary school. My grandfather was still alive and lived in the same house until he too passed away, of old age. He took the responsibility of taking me to the school every morning, where I joined other kids and started my primary education.

My mother had everything planned. Although she knew she was short on resources, she had learned from somewhere or someone that if our condition was to change, it could only happen through my education. She motivated me the best she could, she could not read herself, but she had a strong mind. At every level, she would tell me:

"Jones, I don't know the next step that you have to take, but ask people around you, they know better. I will provide for you, whatever you need." She was willing to do anything for the sake of my education.

Once, I was sitting feeling disheartened as I did not have the necessary books for school, but she said, *"I will sell everything we have for what you need, my goats, our house, or even the last bit of clothing that I am wearing so that your progress does not stop."*

Time flew by and my mother's spirit was still very much alive. I was in primary six; I had been going to school by myself lately. It was a Monday morning, and we all were standing in lines, waiting for the assembly to begin. The headmaster of the school had come in early that day, he had an announcement to make:

"Students, I apologize, but we forgot to inform you that in order to fill in the forms for junior high, we require a passport-size photograph from each of you. Since it was supposed to be brought today and we are already late, we have called the photographer. All you have to do is quickly rush back to you parents before they leave for work and bring the fees for the pictures."

I quickly ran back to my house, my best friend was with me, it was not too far from the school. My mother had prepared herself to go to work on the farm.

"Mother! Mother! Stop, wait. The headmaster has asked us to get this money for the fees of the photograph, and we need it to get into the next class."

She was calmly listening to me and said, *"Okay, wait."* She looked in her apron; it looked like an apron - the women in the village tied a cloth around their waistline and put their clothing on top of it. She took the money out and handed it to me. I was so happy. I began to run back to the school. Halfway there I met with my friend again.

I told him happily, almost screaming with joy: *"My mother has given me the money, where is yours?"*

My friend was rather sad and told me, *"My father has refused to give me the fees, and my mother won't help me."*

I was curious and astonished. *"But, why?"*

He was bereaved and looked at the ground. *"They have already decided that they do not want me to continue after grade six."*

Although my friend had a father and a mother, they still could not give him the money. While my mother was alone, she was alive for the purpose that I became educated.

This was the way life was around the village: the people were resistant towards learning and reluctant to educate their children. I was fortunate, thanks to my mother's vision of education being my way out of poverty, but my friend did not share the same fate. I was permitted to progress to the junior secondary school, while my best friend left the village to move to another nearby town to learn a trade.

My progress in the primary school system had been so extraordinary that my teachers often inquired if someone at home was teaching me, but my mother was unable to read, though she had a lot of knowledge to share. Along with all this, God remained on my side and helped throughout my educational career. Due to this, my intellect developed, and I gained admission into the junior high school, after passing the common entrance exam. My progress had become the reward that my mother had hoped for and deserved, she had dreamt of these days, and I was pleased to have brought them to her.

From the day my mother gave me the money for the photographs, I could feel, in my heart, what my mother had been dreaming of for me for all this time. How brave she had been to make that bold decision, without hesitation, to transform my life, simply by giving me the means to move up a grade in school, before her daily work had even begun - maybe she had to go hungry that day. She made such a difference in our lives. My friend and I were no longer able to see each other regularly, our paths had diverged, and our lives changed. I was now a part of the big race.

We both left the village after some time for different purposes; I went to the city to enroll in secondary school, while he, as I said, had to go to another town to learn a trade. We tried to keep in touch, but our lives were completely different, all because our two families made different decisions. It is not easy for a mother to let her youngest child go far away from her, and I had to do this from the age of 12. The junior secondary school was 45 minutes away from my village, and

I took a local bus for this purpose - another financial burden on my mother, but she never complained. Moreover, she never let me complain either.

At this time, she had no proper, regular job. She would walk through the farms, looking for work, but found none. She diverged herself into doing different things: she bought and sold kola nuts to make some profit that she would save for my education. She would stack them up in a basket and stand near a road so the people passing by would see her. She had no shade and the hot sun would tire her.

My mother learned to make palm oil from the seeds and established a small business. She would trade in cocoa beans at other times. She tried harder than anyone I knew those days, but still could not make enough money to live on, due to intermediaries who would take their goods to the city. We were survivors, like many others, despite my mother's die-hard efforts, we were living on the poverty line, on earnings lower than the equivalent of a dollar a day.

In 1990, according to the World Bank estimates, 35 percent of the world's population lived in extreme poverty, meaning 1.85 billion people were below the threshold of the UN's poverty line. Half that number lived in sub-Saharan countries, including my homeland Nigeria. In my remote, rural village, we had no access to electricity, clean drinking water or quality health care.

During my secondary school career, my grandfather passed away. This was a heavy blow, even though he could not do much for us when he was alive, due to his age. We kept struggling to make more money; the only help we had was from the community - the people were very close-knit, and everyone knew each other well and knew of each other's hardships. The church also looked out for us in these hard times, as my mother was a widow and I was fatherless.

So, whenever the church could manage it, they would provide us with relief. The community was very kind and helpful, they always were, irrespective of the religious beliefs. They supported each other through the worst of times; the times when we had nothing, someone would bring us bread; when my mother got sick, the neighbors brought water and tended to her when I was out at school (because my mother did not want me to miss a single day).

The community was considerate about our situation - a widow trying hard to provide for her children - and they never showed disregard. The farmers were generous to lend us food - yams or whatever they could spare. At this young age of only 12-years, I had learned many things about farming and would often go with my mother to the farm, I knew how to farm cassava, how to cultivate vegetables, and did all the things that I could to ease the burden on my mother.

But she was a strong woman, and instead of taking a rest she would do more work - she never wanted to stop. A single day at the farm was enough to remind me of the struggles that my mother was going through each and every day. She urged me to focus on my studies, I listened; I was her son after all. I could not see her in pain.

After farming, we needed more money, so we went to cut wood and congregated. We then organized it along the roadside to sell to the villagers. This was our way to survive, we were duty- bound to do it to make a living, and to support my education.

These activities did not hinder my education, rather, they helped it to flourish further, as I grew in knowledge, wisdom and ability to learn. My interest in everything made my mother happy.

During my life, there have been many days that were filled with sorrow. After my father died, our main focus was to survive, to earn money to buy food and clothes. Years would pass and we did not buy any clothes - new clothes were a dream, and old clothes, or things that we received from the church, were all that we had. But my mother always saved for my school uniforms.

Our home looked like it had been hit by floods and earthquakes several times (see Photo 1, on page 6). Even when you entered the house, it was like you were still outside: it was open, exposed and hollow. The walls were broken, half of the building had collapsed long ago, and we could not afford to mend it. All we could do was use pieces of sheets to stop the sunlight and insects getting in.

At night, I would sleep with my mother in her room, which was actually outside. We did not have any beds; we used floor mats. During the night it was rather cold, and my mother cuddled me close to keep me warm.

Water was scarce: to get our daily supply of water, I walked with my mother to the riverside to fill our pots. We used the water wisely, so it could last a few days. We bathed in the river and were thankful to God that, unlike other villagers, we never caught any diseases. It was a common trend that many people would fall sick from the same disease and die. This was one of the main reasons my mother wanted me to leave this village, and she saw education as the only path.

I was not all that good in those days. Like my friends I was very mischievous. I would trouble and tease her, make silly demands and disobey her at times. But she was very calm with me, she told me it was all part of life, it was what children do, and she enjoyed every bit of it, rather than running after me with a stick like my friend's mother did. Instead, she spent hours praying to God, praying to him for my future, praying that her son would grow out of miseries, to become wise and helps others. She prayed that I would reach so high that I could leave the scars of my past down below. But these scars proved to only make me stronger.

I remember the time I had done something that made her really mad, so mad that she ran after me but stopped halfway to me and began to pray: "*You are a child of God; you will do good things. I will not use my tongue to say any negative things about you, I will never use my tongue to curse you, Jones.*"

Like all mothers she prayed that I didn't get sick from the water diseases; she prayed that everyone would learn from me; she prayed all day for my safety; she prayed that I didn't get hurt. She never made me feel small, she protected me as a father should, and she loved me tenderly as a mother could. She became everything to me, although I did not have the sense to realize that at the time. She has played an important role in my entire past, she still does in my present and she will continue to do so in my future. She is the motivational force behind my success. She continued to pray for me endlessly; she would stay late in the church to pray for my future. She prayed that the dreams she had seen for me became a reality.

Her untiring efforts, her prayers and her putting me as a priority were the greatest sacrifices. Even though we often did not have enough food to eat or clothes to wear, she made sure that I had everything I needed, that no one made fun of my clothes, and that nothing would come between me and my education - she wanted me to have everything that she could not give.

She counted me as a blessing of God, but she did not know that for me she was the instrument God used to bring his purpose to pass in my life. He, who was always merciful, He, who was always showering me with blessings, He, who was there to protect me in the cold, even though we had less than the equivalent of a dollar a day. She was rich for my future; her dreams were the only treasure she preserved. She was not only my mother, she was also my greatest teacher who taught me to be a good man, a good cook, a good farmer, and a good considerate boy who cares for others. Outside of my salvation, the next best gift God gave me was the gift of a godly mother.

It has been a long journey Mother, but if you can hear me now, I want you to look at your little boy Jones and see how he has grown. I want you to see how much I have changed myself, I don't tease anyone, I help them. I don't get angry, but I spread happiness. Mother look, I am here. I am standing at the height you dreamed of for me. I know you are still worried about me, about my health, about my life, about my future, but don't worry, I have a great God looking after me and guiding me. I still hold that Bible close to my heart. Remember, you bought my first bible for me, even though you could not read it, you knew I could.

CHAPTER 2
Dreams of My Mother

Surely, it is true that a man can never be poor if he has the love of his mother, as she is always willing to give up everything for the sake of her children. She can go through all manner of pains to see her child smile. When we learn how to speak, our first few words include "Mama" or "Ma". We grow up in the most caring arms. She feeds us from her body, once she has gone through the immense pain of birth to give us to life. We receive love from her in an unparalleled way.

They are willing to sacrifice not only their bodies but their dreams for us, and their new dreams are only for us. If someone asks me about the best woman in my life, without hesitation I will say, "It is my mother." This does not mean my wife isn't important to me - there is nothing like the love and affection of a good wife, and I have been fortunate enough to be blessed with one. There is a thin line between the love of a mother and the love of a wife, and while both are equally great, it requires a higher level of maturity to understand the difference.

The love of a mother cannot be replaced with a wife's affection; a wife's affection is something that holds its own important place in a man's life. These are two entirely different forms of love that need to be balanced in a way that keeps a man from breaching the fine line that separates them.

We need to understand and implement the right ways of showing our love. Balance is the name of the game. One needs to maintain an equilibrium in the expression of their love and respect for both women in their lives. Relationships can be tricky, but once you set your boundaries, and do your best not to cross them, life becomes easier. At least that's what I have learned from my experiences. To be fair, I have been blessed with amazing women for both a mother and a wife – understanding, compassionate, supportive, and loving women who I love, respect and cherish with all my heart.

So, when I say my mother is the most precious woman in my life, it has nothing to do with my wife. Rather, it has everything to do with the way my mother did all she could for me and without ever complaining about it. We were always running from hand to mouth, but she was persistent and strong, which motivated me and never made me feel sad about our circumstances. The broken house, the small village, the scarce food and the dirty water didn't matter - I am sure the best gift she ever gave me was her dreams. She dreamed of me becoming a great man, a successful man, a fair, pious, righteous and respectable man. It was late when I realized this, but once I did, I realized I could never thank her enough.

My mother always believed in me and had a gut feeling that I was in this world for a bigger purpose. She had her dreams for me but still, never did she stop me from following my own destiny, my own dreams and passions. We had close to no resources but, the way she dealt with this, she became an inspiration for me. I learned a great deal from my mother, even though she was unable to read or write, like many other people in the village. She did not want me to become one of them.

The day I was born, she committed to herself that she would endure all hardships to change my way of living, and to ensure that the dream she had seen for me, came true. It was the only purpose that had kept her going, through hunger, pain and sickness. She envisioned a future for me filled with possibilities. She somehow knew that if her son was to succeed in life, it could be only done through providing him with an education. She wanted me to have that tool in order to carve a better life for myself.

Although my mother had never been to school, she had a dream for me that, one day, her son would finally go to university. I did not know how a village woman heard the name, but she wanted her son to be a part of a graduate college. Regardless of worrying about how things would turn out if I went to school, my mother was determined to send me to college. It was difficult, given our financial constraints and the expenses involved, but she pulled through. Because her focus was on providing for me and being more concerned about my wellbeing, my mother could not afford a better lifestyle for herself, especially with my father not around. However, something tells me that even if he was around, things wouldn't have been much different. He would have made me work with him on the family farm, while my mother made it her topmost priority that her son got a top-quality education. In my village in Africa, higher education was a vital step in moving above the poverty line, to be successful and if you want to improve your lifestyle beyond the norm, beyond just scraping by to survive.

We had very limited resources and very precise incomes. Like many neighbouring houses, we lived on under the equivalent of one dollar per day earnings, hardly twenty-five dollars in a whole month. To make ends meet, my mother worked all day. The only time we met was in the evenings after work, but if there had been proper lighting on the farms, I can assure you that she would have worked into the night as well.

My mother did all sorts of work for us. She went to work on farms, made palm oil and cut wood to sell. I would assist her as much as I could, and she taught me a great number of skills, which aided me in everyday life. She worked tirelessly so that she could raise money for my school expenses; there was no one else to aid her. Even my other siblings would sometimes return from the city and ask her for money. It was her biggest dream that she often talked about with me:

"Jones, I know one day you will go to the big school, the university. You will become a big man. I will pray to God."

But being a young boy, I had other plans running through my mind. I am not proud of all my plans, as some of them would make my mother cry; the worst feeling to go through. Being a boy, playing games had been the most favorite activity to do with other boys. I played games every day, whenever we had free time in school, in the village or on the farm. Sometimes we would play until the sun set; sometimes I would grow so tired from playing games that going to school the next day would not be possible.

But my mother wanted me to go to school; it was the only thing she wanted back from me. She would stop me from playing too much, as it would hinder my education. As some of the children I played with did not go to school, she would always advise me,

"You're going to play now you should know the child of who you are, you don't belong to any bad group, and you don't join any gang."

She didn't want me to forget the importance of my education and that I had a higher purpose, a good purpose; she didn't want me playing with these children to cause me to stray from my path. She wanted me to always remember my upbringing and not to tarnish our family name by unruly behavior. I would obey her for a day or two, and then run off to play again.

This would displease her a lot, but instead of being angry or frustrated about it, she treated me wisely and she made me understand what I was losing. She understood the fact that playing games were also important for my growth, but she wanted me to dedicate time to my studies as well, to maintain a balance. Due to excessive time being spent on games and other 'useless' activities, my grades began to fall.

This was a shock to her and made her eyes wet. It really was the worst feeling in the world; I had embarrassed her and disregarded her hopes and dreams. After seeing her cry, without saying a word to me, she became quiet and just sighed. I knew that I had to change my ways to make amends, and so I did. I became more dedicated and began to improve myself in school. I spent less time to playing with the boys and instead, after coming back from school, I would go to the farm with my mother and help her with her different chores, although she did not even want me to help her, she just asked me to focus on my education.

In a separate event, this time when I was in Primary 5 and around 10-years-old, a girl had been transferred to my school. She was good, academically, and able to beat me to top place in my class. She even got the award for being the best student for that academic year. That year, I was totally crushed. I still remember how bitterly I cried over the experience. Before that day, I never thought I was vulnerable – at least not that vulnerable.

I was so shattered; it was my mother who put me back together. I clearly recall how my mother tenderly consoled me. She made me realize that my failure to receive the award taught me an important life lesson – sometimes we win and never allowed something like that to happen to me again. The failure of that year made me a better person, a better student. I learned never to take my eye off the ball.

"A mother is not a person to lean on but a person to make leaning unnecessary."

Dorothy Canfield Fisher

I still remember the time when I was just about 11-years of age, I had moved into Primary 6 standard. My mother took me to her thrift society. The thrift society was an organization set up to help people in the village with the financial problems. Women, including my mother, made weekly monetary contributions and took turns to hand out money through interest free loans. Each person may ask for the loan to meet her needs whenever the need arises. The women use the money for all kind of personal financial problems, but my mother, most of the time, requested for loans to cover my school needs. The collections were then given out to the people who needed them. Sometimes, the women would keep contributing money and then loan out the money, interest free, to whomever needed it urgently. I remember, my mother always delayed taking her share of the contributions until we were in urgent need for money for my school supplies.

Now, this thrift society needed to keep records of their donations and needed a bookkeeper, as they could not write themselves. So, my mother talked to them, she said, "my son can do it." Astoundingly, they were all grown women who agreed to take on an 11-year-old boy as their bookkeeper. I tried my best, but still mismanaged the accounts sometimes; I messed up the old records as well. There were times when I could not manage to scribe everything they were telling me, but they kept it in their minds and would tell me the following week when they had their meetings on Fridays.

The main thing that really struck me about this experience was my mother's trust in me. She trusted me with my abilities and believed that her son could become a scribe, an accountant or a bookkeeper, or whatever they wanted to call it. She kept on pushing me and motivating me; she had a firm belief that I could manage their financial registers. As none of the women were able to read or write properly, they became dependent on me. Hence, I became a scribe at a very tender age. You know how people have this image of scribes as being old women or bald-headed men, but this is obviously not always the case. Surprisingly, I was still managing my milk teeth when I became a scribe – quite an achievement, don't you think?

My mom also taught me to dream, and I mean dream BIG. Even before I could dream, she dreamed for me. Her dream for me was so robust that I could not dream less for myself.

She made me believe that there was a bigger world out there that I had to explore. She emphasized to me the importance of higher education as an essential tool to explore that world of opportunities.

My mother had the right skills to develop me into a man of worth. She never let me feel belittled. She had decided that her limitations would not be my limitations. And as I grew older, I realized that her dream was my dream too and the only dream I wanted to pursue.

When I was enrolled in the secondary school, from the age of 12, I stayed in the town for the whole week to attend the school. I would leave on Sunday and return to village on Friday. She worked even harder during these times, and I was not there to help her. If I had wanted to, I could have stayed in the town on weekends too, but I travelled back to the village to help my mother on the farm. I followed this routine until the ninth grade in junior secondary school.

During the three years of junior secondary school, my mother saw very little of me and worried a lot about my health and general wellbeing. So, she would pack enough food for me on Sundays to last the whole week. You could imagine, that's how much she cared for my wellbeing. After working long hours, she would still be able to cook so much for me. She ensured that I had everything necessary with me at school.

My mother did not have much, and food was always scarce. Still, she would pack different ingredients for me, so I could make soup - mostly we ate cassava and nuts, and African yams. It will shock you to know that rice in our village was considered a luxury food item, and usually only eaten on special occasions, such as Christmas and other religious festivals. My mother would take some of the money she earned to get a few measures of rice, to give to me.

When I progressed into senior secondary school (from the age of 15), my visits became much fewer and I saw my mother just once every four to six weeks, but she always ensured I had everything I needed.

During the six years spent in secondary school I missed eating with my mother. Back in Africa, we ate from the same plate. The meals were simple and we didn't use forks. This may come as a surprise for a lot of you, but that's how it was. So, this opportunity to go back to her on the weekends was the only way to eat with her during those years, and I waited for them impatiently. I was also well aware that my mother was getting older and she needed more help from me. So, I insisted on coming back and helping her as much as I could during those two weekend days.

My mother's grandest dream was to see her son study at a university someday, and the funny part about this was, that she hadn't known what a university was until shortly before I graduated from senior secondary school. Well, there is a nice story behind this as well. Our village was located near the roadside, or you could say the highway, though it had raw patches and hundreds of puddles, unlike the ones in Canada or the USA.

This broken road led to the big city, where my siblings and uncles had gone long ago. At that time, Nigeria was under the rule of a military dictator who ruled the country with higher hands. Those were difficult times for my country; there was a multitude of human rights violations. If anyone was seen doing anything against the uniformed men, like protesting, public speeches, or an editorial piece in the newspaper criticizing the military, the next day, or even the same day, police dressed in civilian clothes would come to grab them and throw them in jail.

There were certain groups of people who stood against the dictators and their injustice - the human rights activists, who were clamouring for democracy, and a few vibrant student unions who also wanted democracy, plus an end to corruption and nepotism. In addition, they wanted a better education system for all post-secondary in Nigeria, that the military wasn't delivering.

We were blessed that there was a beautiful university in the nearest city. The university had an active student union, which could be found protesting against the dictators from time to time, chanting their songs of solidarity, one of them being: "*Release our people.*" They would load themselves onto trucks and travel to nearby cities and towns, gather and mobilize other students, and then demonstrate and fight the military government.

My mother grew curious about these people and often asked around. Whenever they passed our village, she chanted loudly:

"*Who are these people? Who are these people in those buses making all kinds of noises?*" People told her that they were students from the universities. "*So, why are they shouting?*" she asked. People told her that they were trying to fight the government; they believed that the government was not doing its job properly and the government had done something wrong, and they wanted to make the government do it right. So, the students mobilized more student groups and, once united, they would protest for their rights. My mother asked them, "*Are there people who can actually fight the government, who can fight for what is right, how strong could they be?*" At this, people would smile with pride and reply to her, "*Yes, they are fighting the government because they know that the government has not done anything for them.*"

At that very moment my mother knew what she wanted her son to be, she wanted him to be one of them. As she said, "*If there's any group of people like that, with the audacity to fight for what is right, then MY SON WILL BE ONE OF THEM ONE DAY!*" That was the moment she had dreamed of making me able to go to university. She had learned that there was a higher place than secondary schools for education and was determined: "*My son has to go there!*"

As my senior secondary school was ending, my mother had no clue as to how I could get into a university, and she told me honestly, "son, after your secondary school, I don't know what next to do for you. What you have to do to go to a higher institution like the university. Ask people and come back home and tell me. I will get the money, so you can move on to that

> "*I cannot forget my mother. Though not as sturdy as others, she is my bridge. When I needed to get across, she steadied herself long enough for me to run across safely.*"
>
> Renita Weems

level." I was so ecstatic to bend to her will. She was determined to do anything; she wanted to move mountains for me, if she knew how, she would find the power. She had her dream for me and I had inherited it from her. It was, undoubtedly, her biggest dream and wish to see me go to and succeed in the university.

Obafemi Awolowo University.
Ile-Ife, Osun state, southwestern Nigeria.

Compare the ambience of Obafemi Awolowo University to that of my home, and you will come to the understanding of why my mother wanted for me to attend such a beautiful campus: she dreamed all that up in her mind. That was the university I was to attend. So, if you compare both sides, you will see that there was a HUGE leap. A huge leap for a person like me who had grown in abject poverty and whose father died at an early age, but still eventually made his way to this beautiful, luxurious academic environment.

I was so excited, her dream – my dream – was becoming a reality! And the dream didn't stop there, she allowed me to travel as well. I remember after secondary school, before I started university, I told my mother I wanted to travel the length and breadth of Nigeria. My mother never held me back; she never stopped me. I realized that opportunity to travel with one of my sisters. She travelled the country with her preacher husband and their children, going from one place to another. I asked my mother, *"Can I go with them; I just want to travel?"* My mother said, *"Yes!"*

Yes, you have to believe it, all this has really happened. And I am the living proof of it; I went from having nothing, to graduating from school, to travelling the country, to graduating from university, to living a comfortable life as a successful physiotherapist in Calgary, all thanks to my ever-determined, ever-extraordinary mother!

After my secondary school years, and after returning from my travels with my sister and her family, I told my mother, *"Mother, I won't be coming to the village now, you have to come and see me because I need to plan and prepare for my university entrance exams."*

My mother complied and said, *"Okay! I'll do that."*

So, now I could not visit my mother very often and my visits home to the village were much reduced. My beloved mother stayed in the village, patiently waiting to see me, and doing her work of farming, cultivating cassava, making palm oil, and buying and selling kola nuts. As this was the only way, we had to make a living and sustain ourselves. It was great news that the government provided a more or less a free education, so we did not have to pay any tuition fees at the university.

Still, there were a lot of other things that people like me were not able to afford without solid support from home. My support came thanks to my mother: she was always there for me, still working and supporting me the best she could.

DREAMS OF MY MOTHER

Unfortunately, I failed in my first attempt to enter the university, but I did not give up - I was determined to fulfil my mother's dream. In my second attempt, I was successful and able to get through the admissions.

> "I wondered if my smile was as big as hers. Maybe as big. But not as beautiful."
>
> Benjamin Alire Sáenz,
> Aristotle & Dante;
> Discover the Secrets of the Universe

My mother came to the city to see me, to see where I was living. I told my mother that, "Mama, I've got my admission to the university." My mother literally danced with joy. She laughed, she danced; she realized that the goal of our lives and her dreams had been achieved while she was still alive. Her son had finally made it to the university!

I still remember the day when the headmaster of my primary school had asked for the money that was up to junior secondary school. This was where my journey really started. If my mother had not given me the money, I would have still been in Nigeria, working hard to make ends meet, learning new skills, and cultivating cassava or making palm oil. No, she wanted something bigger for me, her belief in me was my greatest motivation, and I wanted to make her dreams and deepest desires to come to life. I had seen her suffer through all the troubles that came our way, working hard to be my stalwart umbrella. She was my only home. I can never thank her enough for what she went through for my bright future, for our dreams to come true.

This was the turning point, this was the path we wanted to walk along, and now we were finally here. My mother, throughout her life, taught me that when you dream, sceptics may tell you that your dreams are too big and unachievable, but you must not let them deter you, though you must realize that sometimes you must travel the road all by yourself, and the road to your dreams can be lonely and scary. As you travel this road, the only thing you have is your dream; your dream provides you with the energy and courage to move on. She used to tell me, *"You have the power to dream; you have the power to achieve."*

I always found the words of my mother inspirational and close to my heart. Whenever I felt shattered or lost somewhere, I would recall her enlightened face with a flashback that became my source of motivation to move on. My mother used to imagine me as a highly valued child, instilled with core values of morality, integrity and discipline. She was a strict disciplinarian herself; she used to always improve my human values with the stern disposition of a father and the gentleness of a nursing mother.

"Mama was my greatest teacher, a teacher of compassion, love and fearlessness. If love is sweet as a flower, then my mother is that sweet flower of love."

Stevie Wonder

Her strong faith in me paved the way out for me. Since, at a very young age, she took over these figurehead roles after the death of my father.

Her strong faith in me paved the way out for me. Since, at a very young age, she took over these figurehead roles after the death of my father life returns to you what you give to it. It was only my mom whose influence did much for me to change my inner development as a person. Being a father-less person, I suppose it is natural to take on the most vivid personality in my early youth. It was certainly true in my case, with my mom being the only dominant and motivational figure in my life. Throughout the most difficult stances of her life, my mother had never learned to give up and she encouraged the same thing in me. Hers was simple, yet profound faith in God Almighty, deserved to be novelized with the highest dignity and beautiful values, being deeply embedded within her heart and soul. She always remained somewhat awe-inspiring.

Her high moral standards always restricted me from partaking in any type of wrongdoings. I felt it was utterly impossible for me ever to live up to her! Though, she herself had never attended any school, she always proved to be a true intellect and example for me. The most superlative dream for my mother was not about herself, rather it was all about me. She wanted to see me as a graduate from some top UK or US University, during her lifetime. However, she had never, herself, known what a university actually was.

She was highly inspired by the American standard of living and began instilling in me the same ideals and qualities of character and intelligence. This elevated my self-esteem and confidence. This confidence, somehow, breathed new life into me, it brought a buoyancy that I had not felt ever since my father's demise.

I lived in a village where people were mostly cooperative, average-looking, and fine in heart. They looked upon me as a child, to whom they were always kind – it was just the way things were back then. I, however, was cognizant of their pity.

Even among the average-looking people who made up most of the village population, my looks fell far below the perceived standards of "good-looking." Besides, I always believed that I had no special gifts of any kind to make up for what I lacked in my looks - hence, my lack of confidence. But, my mother never perceived these deficiencies in me. She saw what I didn't – what nobody did – and that's what she held on to. She always kept confidence in me and in my inborn skills.

Her positive attitude and company evidently made me feel that I was a more than adequate companion; she boosted up my personality with a profound sense of reassurance.

Mothers are often faced with difficult circumstances in their lives, that's probably why they are so 'special' and 'divine'. Often, they face some of the most challenging and difficult-to-bear circumstances, which they deal with so gracefully, in a way that fathers cannot. My mother had her own set of difficulties to fight with, the most obvious ones being the untimely death of her husband and the conditions of our abject poverty. She could have said that the world wasn't fair to her at all, but rather she never complained; she chose to stay firm and on course. But, dedication has its own set of limits that, if overburdened, would return to you painfully. Her immense devotion and selfless living to care for her six children, most especially her youngest (who happened to be me), impacted her life positively for us, though not so much for her.

My mother was in her late 50's, with her level of passion and hard work still being the same. She never refused anything difficult in her life, rather, she celebrated every moment by cherishing it whole-heartedly. Nobody could ever imagine the pain behind her every smile and the tears behind her every struggle. I will always be grateful to her throughout my life for this. Her trust and faith in God was a bulwark against adversity. She believed in the Supremacy of God, even throughout the most daunting challenges of her life and always asked for His ultimate help.

She was filled with a beautiful sense of endless faith in God Almighty and was sure that He would always be her sure anchor for her kids. It's true to its end that God makes everything beautiful for His Own purpose and glory. Faith helps us to see the omnipotence of God, rather than the crushing weight of our circumstances; faith helps us to acknowledge the omniscient of God, who has full knowledge of our circumstances; and faith helps us understand the omnipresence of God, He is our present and our ultimate help.

My mother's health gradually began to deteriorate. Though difficult, our village days used to be the most care-free times of our lives. A place with no amenities, lack of infrastructure and void of adequate medical facilities isn't that much of an easy life to live, but even that couldn't shake up the world of extraordinary character that was my mother. She always fought for seemingly lost causes, but she often won in the longer run. Later on, during her senior years, I couldn't feel the same amount of energy in her. Though never expressed, it was all evident in her face.

Though, we don't have any family history for any particular disease, some diseases are purely 'accidental'. What it was and how it happened, we didn't know, but something wasn't right with her. We could see it because, even though she did not belong to or come from a literate, sophisticated native background, my mother was never previously diagnosed with any serious ailments. She rarely visited hospital, because she never got sick. Despite all the signs that this might have been nothing, I couldn't get out of my head the thought that I was going to lose Mom before I got married, before I had kids, before so much. Same was the case with my mom, who didn't even realize that she was gradually going away from us forever.

CHAPTER 3
Her Sickness

M y mother had always been a portrait of sacrifices from every nook that I witnessed throughout my life. She always stood out like a true warrior, an iconic widow, an inspirational mother, and a superb concealer with millions of secret emotions buried inside her loving heart for years. Those emotions were left unexplored. She had never revealed anything less than good with me and for me. There was always a river of secrets behind every silence, a flow of countless tears behind every smile and a rock of hard sacrifices behind every triumphs.

This is what describes a "great mother." She was like a shelter to her family that stood and bore all day long, with no consideration for herself and a promise to withstand anything throughout her entire lifetime. This makes me wonder at mothers and how they are the greatest gift God Almighty has given us on earth and how there is no replacement.

As discussed earlier, my mother had a very tough time in raising me, but she never let feel her burden, ever. Instead, she used to bear everything on her own. She protected me from all those hardships and worldly storms and inspired me to strive for the top, so I could eventually become who I am today.

The successful financial status that I enjoy today, the lifestyle that I am living, the inner peace that I feel right now, the values that I have been brought up with and, most importantly, the dream that I am living, are all the fruits of my mom's prayers, endless hard work and resilience.

I wish she could see me somewhere from the sky how much of a "good man" her little Jones has become today: one of the few, most-awaited dreams of her life that she always lived for.

She had envisioned a future that would be the best for me. One which was void of poverty and full of possibilities. She made this possible with every step she took in her life and by the grace of God Almighty. Though, she never went to school herself, she always had a dream to educate her children with a view to a peaceful future.

After the untimely departure of my father, things weren't the same for her, nor were they by any means favorable - she was faced with widowhood and she had the responsibility of managing six children under one roof, but she took to this with bravery and dedication.

Though my siblings departed the village and our mom years ago, in search of a better living, she never disclosed that pain in her eyes in front of anybody and, instead, she focused her efforts completely towards nurturing my good character.

Educating a child with no financial charms wasn't an easy task, especially for a single mother in those days, when suddenly her marital status did a 360-degree turnaround into a widow, with God Almighty as her Only Supporter. She put her firm faith in God, and she never looked back.

Though the community in our village was kind-hearted and supportive towards my mother, being a widow and I being fatherless. We all loved each other, and they were deeply considerate towards my mother and myself.

My mother, even in the difficult times of life, never cursed or abused me. She refrained from everything that could have possibly hurt my personality at that young age. Rather, she prayed for me at her peak times of frustration.

She has always been a powerful lady that I could look to whenever I felt alone.

Though the beauty of my mother somehow vanished over time and deep shadows began to appear, because of the burdensome duties that she had to manage from dawn to dust since my early childhood, her determination and willpower remained the strongest on earth.

Even in extreme temperatures, on the hottest days, she would work tirelessly on the farms to provide for us. She did everything in her power just to let me sleep well, while she herself spent sleepless nights full of nightmares, but also full of dreams for our brighter tomorrows.

I never ever noticed a single pleat of stress marking her beautiful forehead, or any slight hint of how difficult everything was for her, with me being the only reason for her to smile and her only relief from those depressed long days at the village yards.

She always used to welcome me with that beautiful smile over her face and a gentle pat that only a motherly instinct blessed with God Almighty can usually give, even after painful moments. Not only was this about my mother, I believe it is something universal in every mom... *something heavenly...*

I can still feel that strong pat over my shoulders whenever sitting I alone at home. Those lovely hands turning into wrinkles after harsh struggles, moistened yet dazzling eyes, always cheering me up, and agonized yet serene facial expressions that were loud enough to speak out about the silent chapters of her life. Her expressions covered her anxiety and displayed deep calmness and composure. I can still feel her presence everywhere, even now. Cool breezes on a hot day remind me of her flawless fragrance and motherly touch that she always used to keep with her.

My mother and I used to spend hours later in our lives in discussion, recalling my early childhood memories that sometimes made her laugh aloud. Many times, I used to ask her to share something that she had never said before, something that could make her feel better and calm inside, she always assured me positively.

The sudden demise of my father and the conditions we faced after the event proved to be detrimental to my mother's health. Though, she didn't utter a single word about it; she bore tons of pains and kept her emotions inside.

Seldom did I notice that similar energy within her. She started showing fatigue soon after a few errands. A woman who used to stand care-free all day long just for the sake of her dependents, now needed someone to care for her. But, she never said anything. I wish I could have filled up that empty hole inside her, always.

As discussed earlier, my mother used to trade in cocoa at times, as well as palm oil extraction as a business. Though, traditionally, these are more masculine tasks, she did them happily, even under severe temperatures. Rigorous years of hard work finally paid off for me, but not for her. For so long, she had been the embodiment of resilience and patience, but her body finally started to show exhaustion. It was all her dying-heart efforts that never made me feel neglected.

I gathered, through various moments and events, that my mother was not acting same. Mother had been lousy, irritated, lacking in energy, and had become very slow – everything we never knew she had in her. Since she was not among one of those people who fall sick all the time, it came as a shock to us. It was clear that she was going through some kind of illness. On one fine day, one of my sisters came to the village to visit us. It was then that everything began to be revealed, this came as a surprise, and not a pleasant one of course. My mother had lump on her chest. This lump turned out to be of a cancerous nature.

One day, it was unusually hot in the village. The sweltering sun was harsh on us. On days like these, it was normal for the elderly women in our village to take off their blouses. That's when my sister noticed it.

She observed something strange. There was a small grape-sized mass developing on my mother's left breast. I say developing because when my sister asked Mother how long it had been there, she told her that it had been getting bigger in size, but it didn't bother her. Plus, Mother felt no pain, so my sister overlooked it. Also, back then nobody knew what it was or that it could be deadly. A year later, my sister noticed the lump again. The solid mass was still in the breast, but it had grown bigger still - it was now equal in size to a golf ball.

The condition then alarmed us and my sister insisted that we took Mother to the hospital to determine what, if anything, was wrong. The doctor saw her at the hospital and gave her his diagnosis: she had breast cancer. This was a complete shock to us. The fact that the cancer was already spreading its way throughout her body was still unknown to us.

While not having much exposure to hospitals, I always perceived them as having a certain mystique that was impenetrable to the outside world. Coated in white and parading all the way along the hallways, the doctors disappeared through doorways marked with "restricted access." I have always imagined miracles happening behind those doors. With such an affirmative clinical image, we didn't even realize that our delay to first admit my mother would bounce back on us so badly.

At this point, we didn't have any adequate clinical facilities in our vicinity, so we took a collective decision and moved my mother from the village we used to call home, to a very large city called Ibadan. The city was home to the first University in the country: the University of Ibadan (UI). It was a cosmopolitan town with better amenities by far.

University College Hospital (UCH) is a high-profile teaching hospital at UI. This is due to its advanced medical training and research tools. Providing high quality health care with physicians proficient in difficult surgical procedures and expertise in treating fatal diseases as their core specialty; UCH is a household name in Nigeria. It wasn't the only medical facility residing there, there were many more clinics and consultancy units for life-threating diseases present, though they were mostly unaffordable. The city was truly a social hub, with numerous pubs, General Hospitals, cinemas, stadiums and many amenities, none of which were seen in our village.

My sister was more familiar to the city than us. She took our mother directly to the great Adeoyo General hospital where the diagnosis for cancer was made. The sudden incident was a surprise for her. Despite the fact that the doctors notified us about her critical condition, prior to taking her under observation, she was reluctant to spend even a single night in the hospital. After taking medication for some time, she was advised that surgery was the next step in her treatment. The doctors wanted to admit her before surgery, while performing all the necessary tests, and after surgery, for observation. She conceded to the doctors recommendations, though only after much persuasion.

My mother, as per the expert clinical point of view, needed 24- hour supervision in a medi-care facility where she would be monitored night and day. But she wasn't that type of typical lady; she was truly an iconic woman from God.

Her cancer wasn't easy to treat but then, if I think about it, no cancer is. It required chemotherapy, surgery, and radiotherapy.

Also, cancer is likely to spread and recur. The stage of breast cancer and the grade of the tumor influence a prognosis. Triple negative breast cancer occurs in about 10-20% of diagnosed breast cancers patients and is more likely to affect younger people more among African Americans, Hispanics, and/or those reporting a BRCA1 gene mutation.

Cancer diagnosis is something that comes as a big 'shock' for the whole family, not just the patient alone, not aware about the seriousness of the condition that they would be facing in future. Unlike other syndromes, cancer is an affliction with additional journeys of disillusionment, jolts and pains of struggles which come and change your life completely. A patient won't ever remain the same as he or she used to be with physical beauty all shattered and diminished by the passage of time and the progression of the disease and/or the treatment.

Many cancer survivors will tell you that accepting the diagnosis is a tough one. Always a sobering and somehow mourning moment. It's a life-changing and nerve-wrecking experience with a roller-coaster of emotions. A disease like cancer is something that needs a great deal of inner strength, willpower and determination, to face the painful chemotherapies and bitter medications necessary for survival. All these things couldn't be possible without the moral support from family. But my mom never let that happened with us. At this stage, I was the only one who was still dependent on her.

In the time that elapsed between her diagnosis and arranging her treatment plan, we registered the need to get her admitted to the hospital. She was hospitalized in a facility that seemed, to us, like a "royal palace", with equipment and surgical tools that frightened us. I cringed every time that the thought crossed my mind of the doctors using these tools on my mother. Those intimidating feelings of pain sometimes made goose bumps appear on my skin; I was frightened.

I cried every day, sometimes multiple times a day. Sometimes I cried for absolutely no reason and almost anywhere. I've always been religious, but the strength of my conviction was nothing in comparison to that of my mother's. I didn't want things to slip out of my control for the most precious lady in my life… my 'Mom.'

Slowly, my mother's illness started to impact my day-to-day affairs. During this period, I was actually studying for my university entrance exam in another city so, I was further away from her than usual, but there was no other place my mother would have wanted me to be than in a place where I could prepare well for my exam. I shuttled around to see her whenever needed, whenever I could. My sisters and brother were the ones who really spent time with her at the hospital.

My sister and I were afraid for her. We were empathetic for her but, most importantly, we were hopeful. We started watching programs on cancer awareness and visited some more consultants nearby for a better cure-plan for her. By that time, my mother did not know much about cancer and so receiving the news was more devastating for us than for her. However, she later became more conscious of what she was dealing with when her treatment began.

As mentioned earlier, University College Hospital (UCH) was an expert teaching hospital body with a renowned status as the best in the country. Though it was rather too expensive for us to afford, we wanted the best health treatment for our only guardian.

The changes in her bodily appearance became noticeable with the passage of time, with greater loss of appetite, bruising and unrelenting pain. These became her daily experience, but she never expressed fear or self-pity, she relied on her faith in God and the best medical intervention we could afford. The chemotherapy alone is painful, and the effects of this are agonizing enough to make a person feel out of their mind and scream out for relief. Her appetite had always been a concern for us, but she never paid attention to that. Her faith kept her alive at every point, and God never left her alone; she never doubted that God would come through for her.

Initially, she wasn't exposed to high doses during her chemotherapy sessions. She was given some painkillers and medications for temporary relieve. At this point, she was aware of the ramifications of her cancer diagnosis.

I had graduated from a high-school one year earlier, and I was in a process of preparing to write the University's matriculation examination, upon my mother's wishes. That was the reason that I couldn't contribute much money to her treatment. We didn't have much in the way of savings with us as my mom was the only person earning at that time.

My mother wanted me to prioritize my study plans and exam preparations first; she wanted it that way. Her major goal in life was to see me matriculated. And even then, I was struggling hard to make her dreams come true. Her cancer brought to the forefront a precarious situation for our family, both financially as well as emotionally. We weren't particularly financially secure at that time, and even our relatives couldn't afford to help us much with their limited earnings, though they offered many times.

I was well-acquainted with the devastating effects poverty has on one's life and felt deprivation even before the severe cancer incident. Our poverty at that time became more acutely real and severe by degrees. Without any exaggeration and being euphemistic at any point in this context, my childhood could have been the worst time in my life, but it became the best because of all my mom's blessings over me and my siblings.

The era of my childhood was deeply mired by poverty and here, I mean poverty in every sense of the word: food, shelter, sleep, savings, income, occupation and livelihood. The menace was already there, long before my birth in that region, and I was also forced to become a part of it and had to accept it in full. It had, unwillingly, become a part of my life, like the blood through my veins that I couldn't control, and I wasn't the only one.

Let me explain the literal meaning of 'poverty' in its true sense. Not only is poverty something like the lack of savings or deprivation that you feel, but it's the bitter most feeling of being helpless: while watching your own children and grandchildren die in your arms when there is nothing that you can do for them.

I have been familiar with this level of poverty for a long time. I have felt it and lived it. It's uncontrollable and unstoppable. It never sleeps and never takes a holiday. Poverty has the potential to arrest someone's growth. For our family, it assured that our mother wouldn't ever get the right amount of care that she needed and deserved at this critical stage of her life - the extraordinary treatment for her cancer.

At a time when my mother and I used to live below the poverty-line, she also accepted the challenge and fought bravely against the 'fatal' cancer.

In my little rural life, we had no access to adequate facilities like electricity, safe drinking water, and quality health care, as well as nursing facilities. The results from studies in Nigeria as recent as 2011 indicate that 45% of patients default on chemotherapy due to financial hardship. In 1990, my mother was made a part of that cohort.

The oncologist had decided to begin the treatment at a three-pronged level. My mother had some procedures of chemotherapy followed by a radical mastectomy of her left breast and radiotherapy, in that order. From my current understanding of breast cancer, these approaches of therapy are reserved for 'Stage-3' Cancer and require solid financial assets for a continual procedure which, unfortunately, our whole family lacked at the time.

During the course of her treatment, she experienced considerable side-effects from the chemotherapy and heavy radiation therapy, backed by high-dose supplements and injections. Moreover, her diet plan changed completely, and she was more inclined towards the intake of some bitter juices and fewer calorific foods.

After every session of chemotherapy, my mother used to feel somewhat paralyzed. Common signs included, nausea, vomiting, constant fatigue and weakness, as well as pain. For her, the pain was constant, terrible, and draining. We all were helpless and clueless of what to do for her, other than to give her our love and affection. That feeling of helplessness is terrible to share here, there are no words that can portray our feelings.

Sometimes, life puts us into situations where the entire family becomes helpless, not knowing what to do whenever the pain comes. Pain medication is only the mediator of temporary comfort for the patient, as well as their loved ones.

As the days passed, my mom's condition grew worse; she became weak and thin, losing 10-kg after every chemotherapy session. At one point, she became bedridden and very gaunt. She was offered the best medical services and top doctors under critical observation in Nigeria, but this couldn't continue, we faced the hurdle of unaffordability.

Unfortunately, we couldn't make ends meet for her long-term chemotherapy and radiation treatments. The whole family could no longer raise enough money for these necessary cares. Certainly, many Nigerian-based patients cannot afford costs like these. They and their families often go broke and the patients end up losing their lives, because their families have no money to pay for the treatments.

The result is that, on average, a Nigerian cancer patient is less likely to get regular screening tests, like the pap tests and colonoscopies, which detect the disease in its early, more treatable stages. That person is less likely to be in good health in the first place and, thus, unable to fight back against such fatal diseases, if one occurs.

In Western parlance, our entire family was at the edge of bankruptcy; poverty seemed to have won the battle for many of the families like us. As soon as we realized that we couldn't continue to pay for the treatment of our mom for much longer, we immediately turned towards prayers; one thing mother always had a firm faith in.

In my country, we believe so much in prayer - we have deep faith in what we called a 'miracle'. We learned this strongly from our mother, who was always an embodiment of faith and prayer herself.

Prayer became our lifeline, and, to our surprise, God answered our prayers. Miracles happened, and the health of my mom gradually started to improve, day by day. Though, her physical condition was still not that much better, we could testify that some bits of energy were coming back in her life.

Hope of survival came alive through our prayers. Though, initially, our lives were overshadowed with the thought that hope was completely lost, and the powerful indication made us believe that, apparently, the breast cancer had won the battle, our hope that came back and helped us remain alive in front of our mom.

Hope is a conduit of grace that helps us to continue in misfortunes; if we lose hope, or stop believing in hope, then we lose an essential survival power in ourselves.

No matter how difficult the circumstances could be, I would strongly recommend that when people are going through such tough phases in life, they should never despair and give up hope. Just pray and keep on praying with complete faith and determination and see how miracles happen. I have learned this by myself, not to lose the sight of prayer; it's your faith that will save you and bring you back.

Back in Nigeria, we had no health insurance, or insurance of any kind for that matter, providing coverage against different risks. Cancer is recognized as the most critical health-risk factor that can elevate or cause poverty and loss of social status among the middle class in Nigeria. It's one of the extreme causes behind the prevailing economic crisis of the state. A disturbing repercussion of this is that most of the people that do notice the early signs of cancer but do nothing and other than wish it away.

Rising occurrence of cancer causes overburdening costs of treatment that are putting Nigerians on the edge, because of the average minimum wage. This is merely 18,000 Nigerian Naira (the equivalent of $65.78 CAD) per month as at the time of writing this book, and that isn't sufficient to afford the expensive and prolonged diagnosis, let alone the procurement if the right medical service to manage the ailment.

Cancer is becoming an alarming scourge for the people in poor countries. Both the low and high classes fall victim to the ailment and many of the country's top physicians, who specialize in managing cancer and its complications, have declared the cost of cancer drugs as "too high" and unsustainable. Many of the patients in need of medication, but cannot afford it, then prefer to stay at home and wait to later pass away. Our situation was similar to this in the 1990s, when my mother was battling cancer.

For my mother, though things seemed positive, in an actual sense, they weren't. The disease required much attention and regular therapy exposures and my mother wasn't getting all of these, due to our strict budgetary constraints. I still regret this and deep somewhere in my heart, I blame myself for all this.

I wish I could have been a millionaire at that time, or somehow, at least a working man who could've supported my ever-iconic mom.... I wish I could bring the days back.

A few weeks later, we could no longer afford to continue with the therapy. The pain, initially, began to subside, but it returned after some time. This time, more powerful and painful than before. The initial forlorn existence of my mother that received a mercy spark while her weakened body regained strength, was suddenly in pain once again. Her doctor warned us that if she stopped her therapy, as we decided on doing, she may only have six- to 24-months to live. The cancer was an epidemic within her, and the oncologists believed that the cancer cells had spread to some other organs and tissues. But, and I widely salute my courageous mother for this, she still challenged all the odds and struggled back. Her trust and faith in God was a bulwark against adversity, and a reason that made her survive beyond the disclosed limits of those doctors. God does everything, though doctors are indeed helpers. God Almighty's mercy prevails all over His wrath.

My mother's life transformed and was as a true testimony to God's amazing dealings with those who put their trust in Only Him. She was a fighter – she braved through her sickness and lived for another 24 years, before departing towards her Lord.

Her case was like that of the man by the pool in the Gospel of John Chapter 5:7:

> "*Would you like to be made whole?*" the Lord asked. "*I have no one to help me into the pool when the water is stirred,*" he replied. "*before I scribble my way into the pool; some other people got into the water before me,*" he continued with the narration of his worrisome state. Then Jesus said to him, "*Get up! Pick up your mat and walk.*" At once, the man was cured; he picked up his mat and walked. We declare that this is the Lord's miracle, and it was marvelous in our eyes.

After a few more months of struggle, she had managed to walk around in our backyard, with a stick in her hand for support. Even at that moment of time, she never disturbed us for a single bathroom visit. She was a lady with self-respect at her roots; she always liked to do things on her own without disturbing others. Doctors were amazed to see her like this and declared it as a miracle from God; a thing that, supposedly, humans say whenever they fail after their loss of influence. She even sometimes visited our neighborhood family and spent her time there. She came back and beyond to who she used to be. The Lord renewed her strength as to an eagle and healed her gradually, despite our situation and the silent depression that she went through.

It's all about prayer. The courage, the faith and the determination that we associate with the Lord and how He responds likewise. I wonder why we nimble humans don't realize this? Why we start perceiving ourselves as "superpowers," though we can't even inhale a single breath on our own. I must ask "*Why have we stopped praying today?*"

Sometimes, we think it's too small for God to be bothered with our knock; sometimes, we become impatient and think it's too big for God to handle. But little or big, we all realize, at another time, in all our assumptions, we are wrong! God is God of all circumstances. He is Omnipotent and best Disposer of affairs. God is Great!

God, literally, gave my mother a bonus of an additional 24-years to her life, to witness her grand- and great grandchildren, as well as my graduation, of course, which was one of the 'biggest' dreams of her life.

Her struggles, however, didn't end with cancer in remission. After she regained her health sufficiently, she went back to the village to resume her normal life. At this point in time, I had gained admission to the University and was studying for a degree in Medical Rehabilitation. My mother had gained enough strength to be able to return to farming and she didn't hesitate to start work again, as she knew I still needed her financial help in order to finish my university education. We worked together on the farm to plant cassava, corn, and other crops. I used the proceeds from the farm to buy all the necessary items for school.

The relief my mother felt after her cancer treatment was short-lived. In May 1997, another tragedy struck. She was on the farm tending to our cassava plantation while I was away at university living on campus. As she was working on the farm, a gust of wind blew sand pebbles into her left eye. She rinsed the eye with water and left it at that, few days after the incidence, the eye became infected. The villagers helped with local herbs, but the infection worsened over a period of several weeks. Then, the news came to me on campus that my mother was sick. I rushed to the village to find my mother in excruciating pain and with pus exuding from her left eye. It was another painful episode of my life - the difference this time was that I could do something about it. Within the hour of arriving in the village, I got my mother dressed and I took her to the teaching hospital where I was training to be a Physiotherapist. My mother was seen by the Ophthalmologist the same day. After a battery of tests was performed that same day and during the days to follow, we were given the bad news that my mother had lost her left eye and the Ophthalmologist needed to work very fast to protect the second eye from cross infection. My mother underwent some painful procedures along with a full course of antibiotics, the infection was eventually brought under control, and her right eye was saved. The specialist recommended the use of a prosthetic eye to replace her left eye, but my mother refused.

Even though she had lost one eye, she was full of insights, guiding her children all the way. About a year after this incident, I graduated from the university - she was very proud of my achievement, our achievement. The incident on the farm occurred because she was tending the cassava to earn money for me, to pay for my upkeep on campus: she was determined to do everything so that I didn't lack anything while in school. Her sacrifice had finally paid off. She dressed her best to attend my graduation ceremony. I am forever grateful to her, for her love, resilience, and sacrifice that only mothers can make.

The only good thing that came out of this particular ordeal was, soon after I had taken my mother out of the village to tend to her injury and illness, an intra-tribal war began in August of that year. Many of the villagers were displaced from their homes and farms, and many lost their lives in the conflict; my mother never returned to the village.

CHAPTER 4
Prayers of My Mother

My mother was a woman of faith who truly believed in the power and the acceptance of prayer. Her belief in God and His supremacy was so strong that even in the toughest of times (like the time when she was a young widow on a farm, left to feed and provide for her children on her own), she staunchly believed that God would make everything right. Mother prayed unwaveringly and profusely. A small part of it was, perhaps, an influence of the community. In Nigeria, people believe in the bounty of prayer so much that they believe in miracles – actual-life miracles that happen all the time, if one only cares enough to notice.

My mother prayed all types of prayers, all the time. She believed that each prayer, made righteously, ascended to the presence of God, who never denied it. As I write this portion, I can still hear her prayers. My first insight into spirituality was derived from my mother's devotion to old-fashioned Anglicanism. Morning prayers, for us, were a daily spiritual exercise.

A personal morning prayer always preceded the congregational one. I remember, with fond memories, of my battles of will every morning when my mother would come to wake me up for the Morning Prayer at the church. She would grab my hand and pull me up from our sleeping mat, because I always resisted. I wanted to sleep more, but my mother had a solution for that. In a gentle but firm voice, she would say, *"Son, come with me to church, and when we get there, you can continue your sleep."*

Just like that, I would be out of my bed (actually, it wasn't a bed: we slept on locally-made mat woven from grass) and preparing for church. Such an enormous influence is, I believe, only something a mother can wield over her child. This was the crucible that shaped my earlier spirituality.

A man is nothing without his prayers – especially the ones that are sent his way by his mother. I know I wouldn't have reached where I am today or succeeded the way I have in life, if it weren't for my mother's prayers for me. Like I said, she had big dreams for me. She wanted me to grow up into an educated, successful man, and nothing gives me more pleasure than knowing that I became all that she wanted me to be – and it all happened while she was alive – well, for the most part. The dreams she had for me were bolstered by her prayers.

> *"I remember my mother's prayers and they have always followed me. They clung to me all my life."*
>
> Abraham Lincoln

It was as if she bought her dreams for me from God, by paying her prayers and supplication as a befitting price for them.

Now, I'm not a statesman, but this quote by President Lincoln is close to my heart. This is because I can relate to it. My mother's prayers have protected me, uplifted me, guided me, strengthened me, and helped me find solace after she left us and this world. If it weren't for her and her prayers, I wouldn't be the man I am today. People often find it amusing that I give all the credit of my successes in life to my mother. To be honest, there isn't anything or anyone in this world who deserves the credit more than she does.

This woman – my sweet mother – was my pillar of strength, and even when she was falling apart or having a hard time, she did not falter. No matter what she faced in life, her prayers never stopped. She was always there for me, for us – this solid, resilient wall that did not let us weaken, even in the face of some of the most difficult adversities in life.

I was very young when my mother bought me my first Bible. She, herself, couldn't read or write, but she wanted me to have that Bible. She wanted me to read and understand it, so that I could muster the same kind of belief that she had in God, His message, and His supremacy. That Bible was in our local language and, thanks to the sacrifices and struggle of my mother, I was able to attend school and read the divine message of God.

That Bible was very special to me and I held on to it for many years. It was a treasure for me. Now, I know mothers, in general, are perhaps all the things my mother was - they are full of love and compassion, they put their children first, they nurture them, and help them grow. They pray for them, pick them up when they fall, and help them walk the path of self- discovery that eventually leads them to greater success.

She wanted a life for me that I could not have fathomed for myself, she wanted it so badly that she was willing to sell the clothes she wore, if that's what it took to get me where she wanted to see me. She believed in me and her supplication so strongly that it would have been a sin for me to believe in anything less than that. My mother always said that prayer gives us patience and resilience. It shapes our lives in ways we cannot imagine. I am a living witness to the power of prayer and the reality of miracles. I have experienced and seen things happen in ways I could have never imagined.

Imagine yourself living in a mud-house with a mother and five siblings. A mud-house that doesn't have a proper roof, or proper walls. Our house was broken on one side: it was like we were inside, but still outside, because there was no wall on one side of the house. We survived on a less than the equivalent of one- dollar-a-day income, for the whole family. Imagine, coming from a place like that and ending up graduating university.

Most of the kids in my village couldn't have even imagined ending up the way I did. I did everything with complete honesty, all because of the farsightedness, perseverance, dedication, love, support, dreams, and, of course, the prayers of my mother. I could go on and on praising the woman who raised me and instilled into me the values that made me who I am today – but this chapter is about prayer, and everything I learned about it from my mother, so I'll just focus on that.

Prayer is the purest and easiest form and way to connect and communicate with God. Whether you are uttering a need for help or just pouring your heart out to Him, prayer draws its significance from the fact that God is listening to you. And the Lord said,

"If you abide in me and my words abide in you, ask whatever you will, and it shall be done for you." (John 15:7)

It's like taking an intimate walk with God, where you pour your heart to Him. He listens. Your prayers lay down the foundation of your spirituality. It's a shield that protects you from the struggle against Satan. It is a school that brings you closer to your Lord and allows you ample opportunity to thank Him for His blessings and request Him for the ones you need.

Prayer heals you from the inside, it strengthens your faith and character, and it keeps you away from wrong-doings, and makes you a better person. Look around you and you will find miracles of prayer everywhere, even in your own life, if you care to realize. Look back to the time when you asked God for something through a small prayer and, today, you have what you asked for.

Acceptance is guaranteed. It only takes time. With the right time, effort, and supplication, everything and anything is possible. I learned that from my mama. From a very young age, we learned that we cannot give up praying just because we can't see things happening as fast as we would like them to or the way we would like them to. It is important to realize that God has better timing and better plans than ours.

I remember those times when I would be walking down a dirt road with my mother and people in cars would pass us by. I knew we could never afford something like that - a car. Not back then and, perhaps, not even later, but my mother believed we would, one day. She would tell me that one day I'd be where they are; that I'd drive a car just like them. All I had to do was work hard for it, keep faith, and pray to God. I did all that though maybe not, in fact definitely not, with the intensity that my mother did.

You see, it's easy to lose hope. You are working hard, doing everything you can, and you're praying regularly too, but things just aren't working out the way you want them to, or as quickly as you want them to. You lose hope, saying, "*Maybe it's not meant to be. Maybe God doesn't actually exist. Or maybe He does but He doesn't really love me enough to grant me my desires.*" I've been through that phase too. Not once, but several times in my life. But with my mother around, it was difficult to give up on prayer altogether.

She was such an inspiration, a role-model, someone we could always look up to, and she never gave up on her prayers. She was relentless. If a prayer she made didn't come to realization, she prayed with greater intensity for it. It was as if she was convincing God, reasoning with Him about why He should do what she wants or give her what she wants, and, in the end, He eventually gave in.

Prayers are immensely powerful. Although I outright acknowledged and believed in this fact, my belief in it was reinforced during the time my mother was ill. Now, you already know she was suffering from terminal cancer - something that still tugs at my heart whenever I mention it. There was a time during her illness where her condition worsened to the point that she couldn't continue her treatments. She was already weak with the disease, but the treatment was taxing on her health even more.

Those were difficult times for my family and I, because we didn't know what to expect. If anything, we just wanted our mother to recover, we wanted her to live, to get better. The only thing we could think of at a time like this, was to pray. We had to pray - pray for her health and pray for a miracle.

Prayers were the lifeline that kept us going. They were what kept us from falling apart and losing hope. It would've been easy to lose faith during these testing times, but we somehow managed to keep it anchored and hoped beyond hope that things would get better. Believe it or not, our prayers worked. God listened to them and answered them too. My mother's condition improved, her chances of survival improved. But the battle against breast cancer is a long, debilitating one - both for the patient and for their family.

It did take my mother away from me for good, but not before God made sure she stayed resilient and alive long enough to see her children and grandchildren prosper - to see the seeds she had sown during those long, laborious years bringing us up and shaping our minds for success, grown into sturdy trees that were sowing their own seeds to continue her legacy.

Although no amount of time spent with my mother could've ever be enough for me, I was grateful to have been blessed with the extended life that she lived. There's a part of me who likes to believe that it was our prayers that made this possible, because it's something that makes me feel closer to my mother. After all, prayers mattered so much to her and her belief in their infinite power never wavered – not even once. She was an amazing woman who had modeled the values of being resilient, faithful, and hopeful throughout my life, and all these values were tied together with prayer.

You see, hope and faith go hand-in-hand. My mama always told me that one is incomplete without the other. When you say, "*everything is possible with the help of God,*" you're not just expressing your faith, there is a hint of hope in this very sentence that expresses your faith in the power of your Lord that helps you believe that nothing is impossible when it's Him making the call. Your hope is proof that you have faith; that you believe in something Supreme that is all-knowing and all- controlling. Hers was a very simple, yet profound faith.

Mothers, no matter where in the world they are, face difficult circumstances in their lives, and there are no exceptions to this. The very act of bearing a child for nine whole months and then birthing them with excruciating pain and suffering is more difficult than anything else people undertake. Challenging circumstances can come in the form of being a single parent, abject poverty, loneliness, unexpected pregnancies, divorce, or the overwhelming decision of aborting a child. I am sure that many women today can relate to these situations, where they have found themselves desolate and alone in the face of adversity.

My mother certainly faced those situations. She braved through the untimely death of her husband and faced wretched poverty most of her life. She could have complained that the world, especially God, wasn't fair to her, but why would she? She was a godly woman who faced her difficult circumstances courageously. She chose to stay the course and dedicate her life to care and provide for her six children, in an attempt to make the most of her given circumstances.

I would like to share the story of Jochebed from the scriptures. She too, found herself in a precarious situation, where newborns and infants were being slaughtered in compliance to the King's edict. This woman had an infant of her own and her heart told her that her tiny boy had enormous potential in him. So, despite the tyranny around her, she decided to protect her little boy against the edict of their bloodthirsty ruler.

According to the scriptures, she hid her son for three months until she couldn't do it anymore without attracting the attention of others. She knew if she didn't do anything soon, she might end up surrendering her child to the executioners, but Jochebed wasn't prepared for that. She devised another plan to save her son's life, because she saw what most mothers couldn't see back then – she saw great potential and endless possibilities for this child's future. So, Jochebed did the only thing she could think of. She put her beloved child in a wicker basket lined with tar and floated it down the River Nile– she entrusted her son to God's will and protection.

The child was saved. We are all familiar with the story of Moses. However, it was a decision taken in tough times by his mother that gave the world one of their greatest leaders of all time. Moses had a unique relationship with God in every way. He became the leader of the people of God but what made this possible, was a mother who had faith in God – one who was willing to make the difficult choice of abandoning her child, to rescue him, nestled in a wicker basket that floated to the Pharaoh's daughter.

Motherhood is a blessing that comes with immense responsibility. It is an unsaid promise that a mother makes to her child to love, nurture, protect, and support them. It is not easy, and neither are the decisions that sometimes come along with it. There are sleepless nights and pain, agony, anticipation, and uncertainty, and a range of other emotions that a mother goes through for the sake of her child. If there is anything that can help her survive through all this, it's her faith in God.

For Jochebed, God was all she had, and God did not leave her alone. He saw the agony of her heart and the unwavering faith she had in Him. He was there with her all along, and He rewarded her faith. I could say the same for my mother. No matter what life threw at her, she never left her prayers, she never let her belief in God weaken. So, whether you're a mother struggling to make ends meet to up bring your child, or a woman contemplating an abortion because the road ahead is full of ambiguity, know that God sees your pain. He is witness to your struggles; He is just waiting for you to trust in Him and His plans for you and your child.

Your faith in God becomes bulwark against adversity. The daunting challenges seem easier when you lift your hands in prayer and ask Him for help. Give God a chance and He will give you and your baby the succor you desperately need in this hour. I know this, because I have seen my mother entrust God with every matter concerning her and her children's lives. Yes, she prayed, and He always answered. God's help always comes when you understand and believe in the omnipresence of God.

Being young and living in unbearable poverty sometimes makes you look down upon yourself and your conditions. It makes small children wonder why God has been so unfair on them when He has been blatantly generous to others. It's easy to question your beliefs when you're placing your faith in something you cannot see. Nobody has seen God, but people still believe in Him and His power. You hold on to Him like your life depends on it.

That's what my mother did and that's what I did. Every time we saw someone more endowed and blessed than us, my mother used to say, *"you'll see, one day you're going to own all of that. I know it in my heart, you'll have everything you don't have today."* And now that I look back at this, it's true. My mother was right. I do own everything I could only look at from a distance back then. It was my mother's faith in the power of prayer and my God-given abilities that got me where I am today.

I can never truly emphasize the significance of the impact prayers of a godly mother has in the lives of her children. The prayers she offered on her bended knees were an act of worship, fragranced with the pure love of a devoted heart. Growing up, I was surrounded by a community where parents hauled curses on their children on the paltriest provocation. It came as second nature to them. My mother however, was different. She truly believed in the fact that verbal abuse against young minds sticks to them for the worse, for the rest of their lives.

I never once saw or heard my mother cursing me or my siblings. Even though, I was a mischief-maker during my formative years, my mother never used unedifying words on me. Instead, she made room for my waywardness and allowed me to evolve into a well-rounded personality. There were times when my antics provoked her way beyond her patience. Still, the only thing that came out of her was prayer.

My smallest acts of kindness towards my mother, or anyone else for that matter, elicited prayers from her. It was her way of appreciating my good deeds. Where, for most people in the neighborhood, cursing the child came naturally, for my mother it was praise and prayers for my future. She never resorted to profanity, it was just not her style. I wasn't an easy child. I did things that would have drawn the wrath of almost every other adult in the community, but my mother made deliberate, conscious prayers instead – she wanted me to know that she was asking God for help to make me a good person, inside and outside.

Before I had children of my own, my mother prayed not just for me, but for them too; she prayed for them even before the time when they were born. Today, I look back at how far I have come, and I remember the endless prayers of my mother that have echoed into my present and my future. I am the living testimony of the fact that prayers span over generations. So, what did my mother pray for? She prayed to the Lord to give me a godly woman for a wife. God answered that.

She prayed that my children be godly children, that they would be kind to their parents and others. She prayed that I succeeded in everything I undertook. Simple, meaningful prayers that she put all her heart and soul into, and here I am today, reaping the fruits of her labors. I have everything my mother prayed for me to have. God has been kind to bless me with a mother like that, and to answer all the prayers she made for me.

My mother strongly believed that, no matter what, God would favorably respond to her vulnerability and, believe me, God did – like I said before. Her fervent intercession for her children are a constant reminder that godly mothers are precious jewels of infinite value. Even when you look into the scriptures, it was a mother who petitioned Christ for God's throne for the sake of her children. Who else has the courage to ask for God's throne other than a mother advocating her children? Nothing, and I repeat nothing, is too big for a godly mother. She will ask God for absolutely anything she believes is good for her children. No mountain is too high to surmount, and no challenge too grave for a mother like that. It is the very core of their existence.

This book is really close to my heart, not just because it's about my mother, but because I see so many mothers struggling through life, doing everything they can to provide for their children in the best way possible. I know these mothers go through difficult times, and most of them do it alone – without any help. Sharing my mother's story is more about helping these mothers find the inspiration to make it through. Perseverance does bear fruit, sooner or later, one just needs to be steadfast in their beliefs and have faith in God – this is most important for those who think they don't have anyone, they must remember that they have God looking over them. They just need to ask for help.

In his first letter to Thessalonica, the Apostle Paul wrote, *"Pray without ceasing."* Who was the message meant for? Did he intend it for the Christian men of that time? Or was he commanding everyone, even the busy mothers of two, three or four children. I believe the commandment was for all believers regardless, and it included the Christian mothers too. One of the best ways one can choose to fulfil this sacred injunction, especially in the case of mothers, is to develop a moment by moment attitude of prayer, or like John Piper calls it, *"a continual disposition of prayer".*

It is perhaps the easiest way to instill the habit of establishing regular prayers in young children. A mother's influence on her child is immeasurable. When a child sees his mother praying, asking God for help, he finds himself doing the same, no matter how difficult his situation is.

Cherri Fuller in her book, *"When Mothers Pray,"* explains it this way:

> *"Carry prayer through your day by looking for and asking God for "cues." When you pass your child's school, pray for his teachers. When you wash his sweatshirt, pray he'll be covered in God's protection and love. When you polish her shoes, pray that her feet will take her in God's paths."*

Motherhood is tough. Sometimes children drive their mothers to the edge of insanity. I did, on countless of occasions. At times like these, it is instrumental for a mother to hold on to her patience. Instead of raining fire and brimstone on the child, a mother needs to keep her calm and use the moment to present the child to God in prayer. Prayers work. I can go on saying this gazillion times, because I believe in the miracle of prayer. Before I end this chapter, I want to share a lighthearted quote that I once read, as a remembrance of a mother's prayers.

"There was a Mother's Day card in the gift shop; it read on the front:

Mom, I remember that little prayer you used to say for me every day.

As you opened it, the inside read:

God help you if you ever do that again!"

This simple message printed in the card embodies the real essence and continual disposition of a mother's prayer. There was nothing other-worldly about the message, but the prayer clung to him his whole life. That's how precious a mother's prayer is for people who understand its worth.

My elementary school...

This is the school where I started and completed my
six-year primary education.

The rocky mountain around my village.

Our family farm was at the base of this mountain. We lost the land
and the farm to the intra-tribal war in the city that spilled over to
surrounding villages including my ow

My childhood home

To give you a perspective of where I grew up -
a dilapidated house has been like this for almost 30 yrs.

Our Neighbour's House.

My mother and I began sleeping in this house when grandpa passed away,
we thought it was dangerous for just two of us to be living in our own
house. We usually passed the night in this house and
return to our own house every morning

Palm Fruits.
we make palm oil and other products from the fruits

Cocoa pod from my family farm.

My Mother's Influence

L ife in its real essence, is a journey. Throughout its course, you come across a number of different people. Some people come into your life and stay forever. Others come, stay for a while, and then leave. Every person in your life has a purpose. There's a reason they're sent into your life – each making their impact on you in one way or another. But perhaps the biggest influence in our lives is that of our mothers. Those precious beings responsible for bringing us into this world, teaching us the way of life, and helping us grow into responsible adults.

Those of us who have been blessed with loving mothers are, indeed, lucky. We often do not realize their importance in our lives until it's too late. Thankfully, I realized it sooner than most and, although this tribute to my mother comes long after she has left us forever, I made sure when she was still with us, she knew how much her presence in my life meant to me.

My mother was undoubtedly the biggest influence in my life. She was the force that uplifted and propelled me to where

I am today. She was the one who shaped and sculpted the person I became by being the epitome of godliness – a real-life example of how to live a meaningful life. I wasn't blessed with a privileged childhood, which meant I was deprived of the many advantages other children had; but God made up for all that with a gift that surpassed all the luxuries of the world: He gifted me with a godly mother.

She built into me the very foundations of godly living, empowering me with the ability to distinguish between wrong and right. And she did it the best way she knew how – by setting a practical example of godly living. She couldn't read or write, so reading the Bible on her own was practically impossible for her. I wrote most of her letters for her, because she couldn't write them for herself, but she still made sure all of us – her kids – learned to read and write. Not just that, she even cultivated in us the habit of regularly reading the Bible, so that we were never too far away from God and His teachings.

A mother is the strongest pillar of a household. She is the one who holds everyone together, strengthening them, nurturing them, supporting them. My mother drew her strength from her nearness to God and she never wanted us to miss out on this extremely important part of our lives – religion; belief; God. Everything I know about God, about a godly life, and the significance of family bonds is because of my mother. It all began with her. It was my mother who taught me the importance of living a meaningful life, dedicated to righteousness, and living it with complete integrity, faith and love of God and His people. There hasn't been, and couldn't have been, anyone else who still wields on my life an influence as significant as hers.

We live in an age of moral decadence. We seem to have lost the distinction between good and bad. New generations take pride in living their lives "differently", where they pompously label good as evil and evil as good. A child's first understanding of the word "God" and its significance, comes from their mother. Now, I am not blaming modern-day mothers for it. If anything, I have deep respect in my heart for all mothers, because only they know what they have been through and are still going through to bring up their children in the face of multiple adversities.

I believe that mothers are blessed with the unique opportunity to mold lives every day – when they nurse their child from their bosom, when they help their child take his or her first steps and walk, when they drop their child off and pick them up from school or the playground. Every single moment they spend with their child is an opportunity for them to instill the good values and love of God in their little ones.

Mothers have a place of significance and influence in a child's life. Trust me, I am not the only one who thinks so. The same has been proven in a recent study conducted in Australia. According to the results, about 52% of the people participating in a survey about the influential people in their lives, admitted that their mother was the single most powerful influence in shaping the person they are today. Of these people, 56% were women, 48% were men. This shouldn't come as a surprise. Our mothers do influence our lives. Further results revealed that four-out-of-five people (men and women combined) ranked their mother as being in the top three of the most influential people in their lives. This study, and others like it, expose that it is quite apparent that mothers greatly impact the lives of their children. The question is, however, how they influence them and what this influence will bring upon the child.

Taking the example of my own mother, there is no better way to have a positive impact on young minds than bringing them close to God and His teachings. Helping them imbibe the life and character of Jesus Christ is perhaps the best gift a mother can give to her child – in the form of ingrained righteousness. This is the sacred calling for mothers and they should be honest in fulfilling it. This influence that a mother wields over her children cannot be emphasized enough. It has a timeless, positive impact on the life and minds of the child – an impact that has the powerful capacity to change lives. Mothers are there with their children through everything. They bear the brunt of the child's anger, they stand the tantrums of a toddler and deal with the rebellious nature of teenagers. Sometimes, they even stay put and suffer when their child grows up into a reckless adult.

Being a mother is a tough job, most especially, being a Christian mother in a post-modern secular world filled with challenges, but not without hope.

It can prove to be lonely at times and painful at others. Sometimes it is emotionally draining, yet you see mothers everywhere accepting these challenges with grace and facing all odds with unparalleled dedication and sacrifice. Since we're talking about sacrifice, allow me to narrate the story of an American mother that I recently came across. This particular mother of three was pregnant with her fourth child. Everything seemed normal until the 23rd week of her pregnancy. That's when she was diagnosed with a Stage 4 melanoma. The doctors advised her to deliver her baby immediately and begin with her cancer treatment as soon as possible. At the same time, the doctors also informed her that the baby would have a better chance of survival if she could wait until the 28th week to deliver.

So, this mother, knowing how critical her condition was and how her cancer prognosis would deteriorate, made the selfless decision to postpone her own treatment to give her unborn child a greater chance of surviving. Her unconditional love for her baby overtook everything else that could have influenced her decision in any way. She was ready to sacrifice her own life for the greater good of her child. This is the purest form of sacrifice, of unparalleled love, and, ultimately, the kind, generous heart of a mother.

You know what the best part is? She was not the only mother who did that for her child. Mothers everywhere wouldn't think twice before making a decision like that. In fact, they'd die a hundred times over to give their child a better shot at life. It is this unconditional love that creates the lifelong connection between us and our mothers. I speak from my own experience of the life I led with my mother. Her unconditional love, unparalleled sacrifice, and fervent prayers make me a grateful, humble man. I have been so infinitely blessed because God gave me a mother like mine.

Now, a lot of you might find it amusing to be reading something like this coming from a man - you know, the power of motherhood, the unconditional love of a mother, the selfless sacrifices mothers make for their children - a man could never truly understand and appreciate all that a mother does for her child. Honestly, everything I am writing in this book is just a drop in the ocean. A mother's love is expansive, it gives her the power to brave everything that comes her way. There are numerous ways a mother can leave her legacy behind to her child, but perhaps the best way she could bequeath it upon them, is to teach them the fundamentals of a Christ-centered life. Mothers usually begin early with the spiritual training of their children, in addition to the early childhood education they receive from schools.

However, even if mothers don't do it at an early stage of their child's life, it is never too late to instill it in them - love for God blossoms in the coldest of hearts when the light guides them down the path of righteousness. A mother is that light - the one that shows her child the right path. She teaches them how to pray in the name of Jesus, inculcates in them the value of the word of God and its significance in their lives.

A better life is not just about getting the right education or achieving a better financial status in life, you need more than that to make your life meaningful, to make it worth living. This is something that is fulfilled when you live a Christ-enriched life. That's something my mother bestowed upon me and my siblings. She kept us close to herself and fostered the love of God and Christ into us. It is the same love that helps us keep the memory of our mother alive. She may not be with us physically anymore, but when we remember God, when we seek His help, when we read the Bible, we remember her.

"It is not what you leave to your children that matters, but what you leave in them."

Shannon Adler

I feel I couldn't have explained it any better than in the words of Shannon Adler. You could leave behind a mansion, a luxury car, and a whole lot of worldly possessions for your child, but none of them would really matter if you don't give them the tools to focus and build a heavenly mansion for themselves. Money wouldn't last, property wouldn't last, even the worldly relationships we build wouldn't last. If there is anything that would last a child for their lifetime, it is the love of their mother and the godly values she instills in them.

A true legacy will endure through generations; the one person who is capable and uniquely positioned to build a legacy like that, is a mother. The next example I quote is one we're all familiar with – at least those of us who have read the Bible. This is the story of Timothy and it teaches us a valuable lesson, if we're willing to learn from it. The story talks about the godly legacy that was passed down through three generations. It all began with Lois – the grandmother. The woman conscientiously passed on a legacy of strong

CHAPTER:5
MY MOTHER'S INFLUENCE

faith to Eunice – her daughter. The enlightened daughter then passed down the same legacy of godliness to Timothy – her son. Timothy grew up to evolve into someone that heaven could reckon with.

Godly mothers have an amazing influence over their children. Poverty mired my mother from leaving land, money, status, and various other worldly acquisitions behind, but none of that was important, since the things she actually bequeathed me with – love, faith, and hope – are the very virtues that brought me to all the achievements that came my way. She taught me how to believe. She taught me how to pursue my goals and achieve them without compromising my love, my faith and my hope. My mother also encouraged me to dream – the big dreams – the dreams that inspire you and motivate you.

It's not just the dreams and inspiration that godly mothers invoke in their children through the continual remembrance of God and Christ, the mere act of their influence elevates the status of the mother to one of utmost respect in the eyes of her children. I came across a heart-touching story on www. christianlibrary.org:

A little boy was giving a presentation in his Sunday school class when, in the midst of it, he forgot his lines. His mother was seated in the front row of the audience to encourage and prompt him, if required. Seeing her child in a conundrum, she gestured to him, so he could repeat the words she silently formed with her lips. That didn't help much. So, she finally leaned forward to deliver the cue in a whisper: "*I am the light of the world.*" The child beamed and, without missing a heartbeat, proudly announced, "*My mother is the light of the world.*"

I know, you must be thinking that is wrong on so many levels, and I don't disagree. Jesus Christ is, and forever will be, the true light of the world. But it's the mother who becomes the guiding light for her children that leads them to Christ. And once they find the path of Christ, He leads them through life and through eternity to righteousness. Mothers are the ones who can create this yearning, this thirst and for following the path of God in the hearts and minds of their children. I believe there is no better legacy that can ever be created than this.

I don't know how many of you are familiar with the story of the dying soldier during the American Civil War but, since it's in context with the matter at hand, I feel the need to mention it now.

> Following the end of one of the many battles of civil war, a chaplain came across a wounded soldier, who was dying. Knowing the soldier wouldn't survive, the chaplain took the wounded man's hand and asked, *"brother, what can I do for you?"*
>
> The young soldier replied, "I want you to kneel down and return thanks for me." This was an unusual request coming from someone who was about to die.
>
> "Thanks for what?" asked the chaplain, out of curiosity.
>
> And the soldier replied, "Thank Him for my mother. Thank Him that, because of her, I am a Christian. What would I do now if I were not a Christian?"
>
> - Walter B. Knight

This particular story touched my heart, because it provides the perfect depiction of the influence a godly mother has on her children. Even when he was dying, he asked for nothing but an expression of his gratitude for his mother, who illuminated the path of Christ for him. Godly mothers lead exemplary lives that lay the foundations of their commitment to Christ- centered parenting. They are their protectors and become the first role models a child has, teaching them the values of dignity, compassion, and conviction. A child's earliest learning begins at home and the mother is their first teacher. Their mother's spiritual conviction and acts of compassion impart into their young minds the real meaning of true and lasting happiness.

Children who are raised right, with compassion and spiritual conviction, rarely display the traits of a bully. These children know how to empathize and do everything in their power to alleviate the pain and suffering of others. The loving, passionate environment they are brought up in keeps them away from making people miserable. My mother modeled these virtues for us on a daily basis. She was the one who taught us compassion and unconditional love with her words and with her actions.

She would welcome stranded strangers into our dilapidated home, give them food and shelter for the night, despite being on a tight budget to feed her own family. She was always on the lookout for things and opportunities that were in the best interests of our family. She labored day and night, with dignity and pride – she delivered words of wisdom to us – particularly to me, given that I was the one who spent the most time with her. My mother and I, we shared an attachment that was unbreakable for as long as she was alive, and even now that she isn't, her legacy, all that she taught me, keeps this alive. I'm so proud that I had her as my mother. She was the perfect specimen of exemplary motherhood.

Proverbs 31 – The Sayings of King Lemuel provide us with excellent insight into the expanse of a mother's influence on a child. The chapter begins, "*The words of King Lemuel, the prophecy that his mother taught him.*" Many biblical scholars agree over the connotation that Lemuel was another name for King Solomon, possibly one given to him by his mother. The point highlighted in this particular discourse is the teachings a mother gives to her son in the form of vital spiritual lessons. Lemuel's mother is narrated to be a pious, godly woman. She is the one who teaches Lemuel, or rather King Solomon, everything he needs to know about justice, sobriety, and moral standards to be the king he becomes – precept upon precept. This loving mother even teaches her son about the virtues he should look for in his future wife.

She was a mother who was completely engaged in her son's life – every minute of it. She dedicated most of her time to teach, admonish and instruct him over the right way of life. Even though her man wandered off the path of righteousness and wisdom that she had led him to, he eventually came back to it. Children rebel, countless times, against their mother's devout counsel, but that doesn't mean a mother should stop counseling them altogether. Does God withdraw the air from our nostrils when we don't follow His teachings? No, He does not. He gives you chance upon chance and waits patiently for you to come back to Him one day – someday.

I am a family man and I strongly advocate the principles of a traditional marriage – a marriage where both the mother and the father perform their dual roles in the family. God has created the concept of family to be a wholesome arrangement, where both the mother and the father have their collective and individual share of responsibilities towards their children. Unfortunately, this concept of marriage and family is quickly fading away in the modern society. The increasing number of divorces leads to unconventional arrangements where the child, torn from the family unit, suffers the trauma of custody battles and parenting rights that usually end up in favor of the mothers. Here, the single mothers often become the only constant role model – positive or not – for the children. This is why I have been pressing the need for Christian mothers to realize that they are in an influential position in their child's life – be it at home, at church, or in society at large – a position that is indispensable.

Now, I know how tumultuous the post-divorce period can be for a single mother raising her kids. Wisdom, in such circumstances, demands that these mothers be supported and looked after by the local churches and the community. These new or strengthened connections, alongside lifting some of the burden off the mother's shoulders, can care for the children, bringing them closer to God. This is the care that goes beyond the monetary support, child support or tax benefits, or whatever. As difficult as it is for the parents, divorce has a negative impact on the children too.

At this time, more than ever, these children need love, support, care, and someone to tell them that Christ is looking over them; that everything will be all right. It's the mothers who take the initial mantle of guiding their children's moral compass and, possibly, become their sole source of inspiration – for better or for worse. And to make sure the mother fulfils these roles efficiently her spiritual welfare is imperative. The church can play a significant part in improving the scenario of single motherhood.

My mother became a widow and slipped into single motherhood thirty-seven years prior to her death. It was at that time that she became the most immediate and powerful influence in my life. Day in, day out, she inspired me with her fortitude and her grace - she stirred in me the love of God, she inspired me to dream big and to chase those dreams no matter how unrealistic they seemed to be back then. She made sure she equipped me with all the hope, courage, motivation, and education I needed to accomplish everything she, or my father, could not achieve in their lifetimes. She made me look towards and work for a brighter future. Seeing me achieve all that I did during her lifetime was perhaps the biggest achievement for my mother, and she was so proud of it. She was proud of me.

Had she been alive today to see where the seed she sowed in me as a child have grown into, she would have been on cloud nine, exploding with pride. That is my mother's legacy. My mother was special. Maybe to the onlooker, she may have seemed just like every other mother doing whatever they can for their children's bright future, but for me, she was the best there could have ever been. And isn't that exactly how it is? For every child, their mother is the best mother in the world. Why? It's because it's the mothers who go through all the pain, the sleepless nights, wiping tears and kissing injuries to make them all right. It's the mothers that inspire, that show the light, guide the way, correct the wrongs, teach the meaning of love, and make you believe that even when the world feels empty, there is always one person who will never stop loving you. They are the person who promises to dedicate every moment of their life to your wellbeing from the very moment you're born – that person is none other than your mother!

CHAPTER 6
A Mother's Love

So, how many of you know about the time when God created mothers? It is often narrated that when God was creating one of his most precious creations – mothers - He was already into the sixth day - "overtime." Imagine God and overtime – ridiculous, right?.

An excerpt taken from "When God Created Mothers," by Erma Bombeck (2005), provides a wonderful and insightfully accurate depiction of what it is to be a mother:

So, on the sixth day one of the angels appeared by His side and observed, "You're doing a lot of fiddling around on this one."

"Have you read the specifications on this order?" God asked. "She has to be completely washable, but not plastic. Have 180 moveable parts... all replaceable. Run on black coffee and leftovers. Have a lap that disappears when she stands up. A kiss that can cure anything from a broken leg to a disappointed love affair. And six pairs of hands."

The angel was taken back, she shook her head in denial saying, "*Six pairs of hands no way.*"

Somehow, that wasn't the only complication God faced with this one.

"*It's not the hands that are causing me problems, it's the three pairs of eyes that mothers have to have,*" God stated.

"*That's on the standard model?*" the angel inquired, definitely baffled. God solemnly nodded.

"*One pair that sees through closed doors when she asks, 'What are you kids doing in there?' when she already knows. Another here, in the back of her head that sees what she shouldn't but what she has to know, and of course the ones here in front that can look at a child when he goofs up and say. 'I understand, and I love you' without so much as uttering a word,*" God explained.

The angel could see this specific order will take longer than anticipated, so she gently touched the Lord's sleeve saying, "*God, get some rest tomorrow* "

But before she could finish, God intervened stating, "*I can't, I'm so close to creating something so close to myself. Already, I have one who heals herself when she is sick, can feed a family of six on one pound of hamburger and can get a nine-year-old to stand under a shower.*"

The angel, hearing all this, had her eyes wide with wonder. She circled the model and couldn't help but notice, "*It's too soft,*" she said almost disappointed.

"*But tough!*" God countered, in an excited tone. "*You can't imagine what this mother can do or endure.*"

"*Can it think?*" the angel was curious now.

"*Not only can it think, it can also reason and compromise,*" said the Lord, His voice proud.

Mesmerized, the angel bent forward and traced her finger across the mother's cheek. "*There's a leak,*" she announced. "*I told You, You were trying to put too much into this model.*"

"*That's not a leak, that's a tear.*" The Lord replied. "*What's it for?*" the angel inquired.

"*The tear is for pain and sadness, joy and pride, disappointment and loneliness,*" God said, puzzled.

"*You're a genius,*" the angel hailed.

"*Except, I didn't put it there,*" God replied somberly.

Aren't mothers just too good to be true? - their love is incomparable. It doesn't begin when a child is born; it begins way before that. This mother lives her days in anticipation until the moment she conceives her child – she is already woven into this spell of love by just longing to have a child of her own to hold, love and cherish for a lifetime. This unique love affair between a mother and her child becomes the most important and celebrated pre-occupation for a woman blessed with motherhood.

When a woman conceives, it is the moment when God combines two hearts together, beating in perfect harmony and creating a bond that no man can even begin to imagine or experience. The child she carries in her womb finds sustenance through the umbilical cord that connects the mother and child together. Even though the umbilical cord is severed at the time of birth, the connection between a mother and her child lives on, in the form of an incorporeal cord woven together with unconditional love and affection. This permanent cord is so strong that it lasts a lifetime, keeping both the mother and child attached to each other for life. It's a love without measure; a love that knows no bounds.

The book "*Can a Man Live without God?*" by Ravi Zacharias (2004), narrates a befitting parable that crisply, but perfectly, captures the real essence of the love of a mother.

The story tells of a young man from the village who grew an affection for a woman who lived in the neighboring village. Proclaiming that his love was genuine, he sought the woman's hand in marriage. The woman, however, knowing the extent of his love, took to manipulating his feelings for her own gain. For her, it was a game. She was always demanding a proof of the love he had for her. Then, one day, when at last she had used every possible ploy she could think of, the woman then demanded the impossible. She said, "*If you really love me, I would like to be confident that it is an unrivaled love. To prove that, I ask you to take your mother's life and bring her heart to me as a trophy of my victory over your love for her.*"

That day, the young man was shattered, stricken with grief and confounded at his only option. He couldn't bear to lose this woman and he would have hated to see his mother all alone. So, in a frantic fit, he killed his mother and removed the heart from her body. He then took the trophy and ran as fast as he could to present it to the girl of his dreams. All this while, grief ate at him, tormenting his mind. He was running through the woods when he suddenly stumbled on something and fell, the heart bouncing off from his hand and landing somewhere in the undergrowth.

The man got back to his feet and frantically rummaged the ground searching for the heart. He finally found it and picked it up. He was dusting his knees off, when he heard a concerned voice coming from the heart, asking, *"Son, are you hurt? Son, are you hurt?"*

Wasn't that graphic? It brought tears to my eyes when I first read it – a touchingly beautiful demonstration of the love a mother has for her child. No matter how rough the circumstances become, no matter how distant the child gets, a mother never stops loving her child. Through the highs and lows of life, the good and bad, a mother sticks around, looking over her children like a guardian angel. She is always there for them.

When a child is young and vulnerable, the mother stays around to nurture them and help them grow. When the child enters the challenging years of the teens, when their emotions are all over the place like a roller coaster – when their hearts get jilted and they can't seem to contain the overflowing sentiments – the mother is there to hold them, comfort them, and encourage them to move forward. Mothers have this other- worldly ability to discern our high points from our low points, even without us mentioning a word about it to them. They just know how to respond in a given situation – it comes to them naturally. They are there to comfort us, nurture us, encourage us, love us, and take our fears away. With our mothers by our side, we are never alone.

A mother's love knows no bounds – it is infinite. During my early years, growing up in the village, I fell ill with a peculiar sickness – an intestinal tapeworm infection that led to excruciating pain in the stomach. The illness was accompanied with nausea, weakness, and vomiting, caused by malnutrition. The infection was caused by contaminated water and food sources we were exposed to in our village. The hygiene conditions were deplorable: you could see fecal waste lying around out in the open across the neighborhood.

There was no proper waste management system, and all of this took its toll on our health. Whenever, I suffered a tapeworm attack, it stayed for days, making me suffer from excruciating stomach aches and sleepless nights. Even when these tapeworms were excreted – in fairly large quantities – the pain did not subside. Nothing helped to take the pain away – nothing, but my mother's loving touch.

I remember how she used her soothing hands to massage my tummy, relaxing me in the process and luring me into the world of sleep. She couldn't sleep until I found rest. She would just carry the burden of this illness with me, praying for my comfort and seeking effective remedies for my condition. The love and care she showered me with is beyond the explanation of words. Tapeworm infections remained my constant companion until the age of 12; that's when I left the village and relocated to a nearby town to attend junior secondary school. Back in the village, before I even turned 12-years-old, I had already lost friends to infections that were seemingly not life threatening. One of my friends died of an ear infection, there were others who were victims of minor accidents, yet succumbed to injuries because our village lacked the emergency health care, or any healthcare for that matter.

Ours and the surrounding villages were plagued with instances of ringworm infections and cholera. My father was fifty-three-years-old when he died. I was only four then. He was always a smoker, plus he suffered from asthma. Medical evidence showed that he had all the symptoms of a Chronic Obstructive Pulmonary Disease (COPD). Sometime in May 1976, my father suffered an asthma attack that led to sudden blindness in both his eyes.

I don't remember much from that time, because I was too young when all this happened. What I narrate here are the events as described by my eldest brother:

We lived in a superstitious society and the family initially connected our father's blindness to witchcraft. However, a later examination of our father revealed the scientific cause of his blindness - it was a common occurrence in cases of COPD and asthma. It is caused, mainly, due to hypoxemia (depleted oxygen levels in the blood), especially when a comorbidity condition like high blood pressure or diabetes exists.

Back then, there were no indications that my father had hypertension or diabetes. We had to move him from the village we lived in to the nearby big city for specialized medical treatment. His medical condition pushed him into depression and he never improved. He passed away in September 1976. From the day he died to thirty-seven years of her life after that, my mother remained a widow, and remained strong. She was the embodiment of love – unconditional love – for her children, and even the people who knew her and were close to her heart. She had it tough, but she never resorted to blaming anyone for her situation. Instead, she embraced it and did everything in her power to propel her children towards a brighter future.

Hers was a love that was profound and genuine. There is a preponderance of social scientific research that has studied the significance of the unconditional love and affection of a mother on her child's development. In a piece titled, *"The Real Root Causes of Violent Crimes,"* researcher and author Patrick Fagan (1995) points out that from the earliest exposure to a mother's intense affection are laid the foundations of the conscientious and moral empathetic development of the child. When a child's emotional connection with his or her mother in the early years of life is disrupted in any way, there is a possibility that it would harm the child's capacity to form emotional attachments with others. The child would grow up to be skeptical and antisocial – detaching him- or herself from the basic human need to socialize. A child who faces separation from their mother, between the ages of six-months and three-years, may have to deal with long-lasting, negative impacts on their emotional and behavioral development. That's how powerful the emotional bond is between a mother and her child – one can't even begin to imagine!

Modern-day motherhood is, more or less, caught up in a spiral of contradictions. The rising phenomenon of feminism has, to some extent, distorted the value of motherhood, viewing it as debasing for the female identity. On the flip side, there are traditionalists who believe that motherhood is the real essence of the female identity – like motherhood completes a woman. *To each their own*: I do not wish to debate on the ways motherhood is woven into the female identity. I do, however, know or have seen women doing great work, be it for their families or for the world at large. You know what the best part is? Not all of them are mothers, neither by adoption nor biological procreations. The thing that matters most is that these women are living meaningful lives full of joy, as women – their own female identity – that cannot be taken away from them, regardless of whether they experience motherhood.

However, when motherhood does befall a woman, or she takes up a maternal role, one cannot just separate their role as a mother – at least not without shaking the foundations of her family. This is something that comes naturally to a mother, if she is accepting of the role wholeheartedly. Motherhood adds a whole new world of responsibility to the joys to a woman's life.

She has the immense power to influence and nurture precious lives and the young minds of her children. We see mothers, even today, giving up fulfilling careers to stay at home and do justice to their role as a mother. Then there are those mothers who, unapologetically, juggle jobs, homes, and their roles as responsible mothers to perfection. Do any of them have to apologize for choosing a path different from the others? Absolutely not.

Motherhood may bring a woman to a point where she must give up a lot of things for the sake of her child. But whatever her decision, she doesn't have to explain her choices to anyone. All that matters is that these mothers are content with their personal paths. In the book *"The Cultural Contradictions of Motherhood,"* Sharon Hays (1998) points out the existing contradictions in the ideologies of motherhood that exist in societies in general. These ideologies coexist. Where, at one end we have the warm, nurturing image of a mother dedicated to the demands of her family, on the other, there is the career- oriented woman, who is cold and competitive, or as she is perceived by society.

Both these types of women may have different ideas when it comes to child rearing – both traditional and contemporary – but that doesn't make either of them better than the other. It is society's perception that labels one mother as warm and nurturing and the other as cold and competitive, just because the latter chooses to bring her child up in a way perceived as "unconventional" by onlookers.

The conflicting ideologies of motherhood will remain where they are in the world view. However, for Christian mothers, these ideologies shouldn't matter much. What matters is that the mothers place their trust in God and look upon motherhood as a divine task assigned to them by their Lord. It doesn't matter whether this mother is a professional or the stay-at-home type.

My mother faced similar scenarios and viewpoints after my father's death, but she did not pay much heed to them. She took the role of both mother and father upon herself, trusting God to show her the way to cope with this complication in her life, and He guided her. She wasn't perfect at the job; she made mistakes and she learned from them but, you see, perfection was never her goal. It was her dedication to her calling – her dedication to motherhood. She may have been a flawed woman, but as a mother, she was the epitome of love, resilience, courage, sacrifice, and commitment.

It was her hard work and determination to her calling that taught me the virtue and value of being committed to one's work. And blessings were bestowed upon us as a result of this. For a Christian mother like mine, motherhood is more than just a worldly role, it is a divine calling from God which should, in every way possible, be carried out with utmost faith and dedication. The gift of mothers was bestowed upon society to give families and communities strong moral foundations.

Mothers were sent to raise compassionate, honest, civil, and honorable young men and women who live by and carry the values of society and communal harmony forward. Like Patrick Fagan (1995) states,

"The mother's strong affectionate attachment to her child is the child's best buffer against a life of crime."

While growing up, I did not participate in any organized sport or lessons of art or music etc. Why? My mother never took me to anything like these because, honestly, such classes were not available in or around our village - the society in which I grew up did not consider these activities as an integral part of learning or parental responsibility. So, I learned soccer by playing it with the older boys, some of them even twenty- years older than me.

I learned swimming in a river that flowed through our village. We (my friends and I) went fishing all the time, because fish were our prime source of protein. Sometimes I wonder if I would have been able to do all that, and learn so much on my own had my mother served it to me without me having to put in the effort to get it. Perhaps not. While learning all this, I even learned to cook - my mother wanted me to. She was the role model I followed and looked up to.

The pure, boundless, enduring, and sacrificial love of my mother was enough for me to last more than her limited lifetime. My mother's heart held such an abundance of love that everyone who knew her, or even met her for the first time, felt it. She showed genuine affection for the weak, the poor, the neighbors and even for wandering travelers. Her love for me was so much that it gave her the strength to let me go, as I moved far away from her to allow me the pursuance of my aspirations and goals. She taught me how to share, how to care, how to give, how to love, and how to be the man I am today!

CHAPTER 7
Motherhood is Missional

"The most important gift you can give your child is to help them begin a walk of faith with the God of the universe. From the moment your children arrive in your home, you are teaching them how to see the world, what to consider important, what to seek, what to love. As a mother, you have the opportunity to form your home and family life in such a way that God's reality comes alive to your children each day."

Sally Clarkson

Mother is not just a biological 'someone' who gives birth to another life form. Instead, it is every woman who has nurtured a living soul and played a part in his or her successful growth.

Recently, my wife and I went to a Christian school for a parent interview, as we were hoping for our daughter to attend that school in grade-one. The interviewer questioned us about our faith, individual understanding of Christian living, expectations about our beliefs and why we would prefer a Christian school.

We answered all these questions thoroughly, giving our best. By the end of the interview, we were asked about our involvement in the local church. I went first and replied to the questions in detail. I told her that I try to assist my Pastor in every way possible, and he often asks me to teach "search the scripture" on Sunday mornings. Further, I said that I also help in leading the home-caring fellowship on Sunday evening at a member's house, and sometimes assist in supporting the outreach program on campus; summarizing that I do all the work that my Pastor assigns me.

After completing my answer, I looked up to my wife to answer her part of the question, to which she became a little hesitant. After a time, she mustered up the courage and said, *"With three little children, my hands are full at home."* When the interviewer heard this, she looked up and said something beautiful, inspirational and eye-opening: *"With three little children, you have already found a place of ministry for God and for Church, which is the whole truth."*

What she said was something most Christian mothers often forget. They forget that the single most important soul they could win over, is their children. Yes, the children in the care and attention of Christian mothers have the potential to get closer to Christ sooner than expected. A mother's love and affection, and God-centered upbringing functions like a magnet that draws the children closer to Christ.

In 1 Samuel, Hannah went through great hardships of not being able to conceive a child and when gifted a child by God, she nurtured Samuel and kept her promise to God by returning Samuel to serve in the temple. She also taught him about the God of Israel: Yahweh.

Even after living among the children of Eli, under their corrupting influence and in full view, Samuel never adapted such bad influences and was never corrupted like them, since he was closer to God. Later, he was acknowledged as one of the great prophets of Israel.

All of this happened because of the grateful and sacrificial nature of Samuel's godly mother who was barren and desperately requested the Lord for a child, making a promise of giving the child back to God. Hannah proved herself as a living example of sacrificial motherhood; there is, perhaps, no occupation in the world which is as intrinsically dedicated as motherhood.

This is why motherhood is missional and serves as a place where God's miraculous love is relived again. It was the objective of God to choose motherhood as a means of showering His love and blessings on the world, over and over again. Through motherhood, God brought children closer to Him spiritually. Motherhood worked as one of its kind channels to let God perfect His creation, by preparing them for the Kingdom's work and service.

This can be illustrated by Saint Timothy's life. Apostle Paul sincerely accredited the strong faith of Timothy's mother, Eunice, and his grandmother, Lois, which led to the emergence of an influential pastor in young Timothy.

We all know that the Christian faith isn't inherited, which is why it is not easy to simply make the children come to faith just because their mothers are followers of Christ. However, with the assistance and grace provided by Christ, a Christian mother can meticulously strive for the conversion of their children to the faith. This faith will serve as an amazing experience for their children during which they'll eventually get close to Christ. In the case of Timothy, his mother and grandmother diligently spent their lives serving Christ and communicated all of that to him. What an enchanting experience that would be, witnessing our children come to faith during the most tender age of their lives, eliminating the fact that they have to undergo the morally corrupt system of the world in which they are brought up.

Another influential example to the missionary of motherhood would be of Amy Carmichael (1867-1951), who accepted her fate as a childless-woman who could not have children of her own. However, she worked towards nurturing those children who were unwanted and abused in many ways. Through the love of Christ, Amy Carmichael became an inspirational mother-figure, and worked tirelessly as a missionary in India. She spread the word of the Kingdom and played her part by sharing the undying love of God to the world.

The only sign that was carved on her grave stone was the word "Amma," which stands for "Mother" in the Tamil language, where Amy spent most of her life. Amy's legacy demonstrates that one doesn't have to bear a child of their own to spread the love and message of Christ to the new generation. This can be done by women to children who are destined to receive love from a mother-figure.

Over the fifty years she spent in India, she took care of hundreds of unwanted and abandoned children. She was a loving and caring mother to them all. A mother who nurtured and inspired them towards the teachings of Christ and through expanding the boundaries of the gospel. Nothing could be more stirring than this way of showing the love of God.

On this, the Bible reveals to us that, *"for God so loved the world that He gave His one and only Son, that whoever believes in Him shall not perish but have eternal life.*" (John 3:16, New International Version). This meant that God sent Christ for our redemption, and in an attempt to save the mankind from the judgment to come, Christ accomplished the work for our full salvation. Even then God showered His blessings on us. He blessed us with Christian mothers who have a purpose to fulfill within their lifetime – the purpose of adorning the gospel with their representative living style, prayers, and nurturing the children into spiritual beings.

I have noticed that Christian mothers take the upbringing and conversion of their children very seriously - just like my mother - and see it as the predominant purpose of their mission. They will always make sure that their children have a full, in-depth knowledge of Christ by "*all means necessary*" (Elesha Coffman, author of "*The Christian Century and the Rise of the Protestant Mainline*," Oxford University Press).

I still remember the time when my mother bought my first Bible. I was around 12 when she gifted me my very own Holy Bible, which I carried around with me everywhere. I loved it with all my heart, and used it so much that later, I had to re-bind the back cover. It was a cherished possession for me, something which always reminded me of my mother's love. I kept it close to me until one day, in December of 1990, I had a personal encounter with Christ.

After I devoted all my love and emotion to Christ, and gave Him my heart, He became my ultimate Lord and savior and later I served Him as a witness. A witness of Jesus Christ in the most significant manner is to keep in mind a viable and personal testimony that He is the One and Only divine Son of God: the true Savior, and Redeemer of the world.

One day, I witnessed all of that to a new friend of mine who, not long after us meeting, expressed the desire to present his heart to Christ in an unpretentious way; he was enthusiastic to learn more about Christ. The only stumbling block in his way was his inability to read in the English language. He could only read in his, and my, local language (in which my copy of the Bible was written) unlike me, who graduated from secondary school and could read and converse fluently in the English.

At this time, I made a heart-breaking sacrifice of giving him my most precious Bible. But, surprisingly, knowing that giving away my valuable Bible served a greater purpose, I didn't think much about it and was actually a source of joy for me. After all, he was the one who had just volunteered to bring himself closer to Christ. I somehow recognized that this was destined to happen and was a part of my mother's legacy.

I understood how she embedded the love of God in my heart and soul by giving me my very first Bible.

My mother never stopped praying, and tried to pray in the best way possible, even though, at that time, we weren't taught thoroughly about the concept of being born-again in the Anglican Church. However, she worked hard to enlighten my knowledge in accordance with the level of light she had shining from her. Even after lacking in knowledge, she continued to motivate me towards the miracles of Jesus Christ. I think that mothers across different cultures and creeds have an incredible amount of inspiration waiting to be unshackled and released on their children.

Thomas Edison once said, "*my mother was the making of me. She was so true and so sure of me; I felt that I had someone to live for - someone I must not disappoint. The memory of my mother will always be a blessing to me.*" This saying is one of my favorites as every single word that Thomas Edison said reminds me of the extremely loving and caring nature of my mother, her legacy, and the missionary of motherhood. My mother was not well versed or educated in the conventional sense, but she made the best of her limited knowledge to shower me with the blessings of Jesus Christ. Now, a part of her breathes inside of me.

When a woman embraces motherhood, she gradually unleashes her full potential towards the spiritual upbringing of her children to make sure that her teachings have a positive impact, not just on her family, but on her children's entire generation. Sufficient amount of learning through mothers is required by children which will ensure the safety of the future generations, as the religious base of the children is dependent on this being strong enough. The ripples of the motherly influence are felt in the future generation; this is evident in my life.

My mother prayed for me, day and night. She always wished for my life to get better, and never stopped dreaming of seeing me as a prosperous and successful human being, in every aspect of life. This belief of my mother's brought me closer to her and to Jesus Christ. Luckily, this love for Christ will make its way into the hearts and souls of my children in the future as well.

When we talk about taking the charm away from the beautiful gift of motherhood, one thing certainly stands out, this is mocking your child and making fun of their flaws. Although sarcasm may fit well with people who are well past puberty, it certainly does not fit with anyone in the younger age bracket. You have to be very careful in making a joke with a child. They are sensitive little beings whose hearts are pure. They may not be able to fathom if you throw any sarcastic remark their way. A mother's sarcasm may have been intended to make light of a situation, but it may sting her child's soft heart.

Children are always affected by anything that comes their way, which is also the reason why you would never let your kids be exposed to any kind of violence. God has instilled upon children the urge to be loved and accepted. They want positive attention from their parents, and when they do not get it, they try to take it through acting out in different ways.

When a child is faced with a sarcastic remark, especially from a person they trust the most - their mother - they will definitely be hurt by those comments. Even if you explain to your kid that it was a joke, it would still leave a lasting impression on their fragile little minds. For a child, it would come across as cruel, that their mother is making fun of their drawbacks. This can also lead a child to grow up to be an adult and think of himself or herself being still lacking in the thing that their mother made a sarcastic remark about. Hence, it is important to know that your kids must not be made a target of your sarcastic remarks, no matter how good joke you may think it would be.

If your child is indeed breaking any rules, or underperforming in his or her studies, or even doing something that they shouldn't, then all they need is guidance from a mother's side. Her loving and kind nature, and the way a mother can explain to a child right from wrong, that is what the child will listen to and make a point to follow. Instill the belief in God of your child and tell them how God has blessed them with so many wonderful things. Tell your children how wonderful they are and let them know how they are going away from those gifts that they have been blessed with by doing something that is wrong or could be improved for the better. A sarcastic remark may only have the child think that their mother is not fond of them. This may result in the child being pushed away from the mother and no mother who loves her child would want that to happen. She would always want her child to love her in the same way she loves them, and just the way God loves his children. To a child, a mother always needs to be a hero with the skills of patience, kindness, and compassion that have been granted to her by God.

Heroic acts by Samuel, Lemuel, Moses, and Timothy will always serve as an ultimate form of motivation towards serving Jesus Christ. One should never forget that behind all their accomplishments, were heroic actions of faith by their mothers. The efforts of their mothers to bring their sons closer to serve humanity can never go unnoticed. If you look carefully, you will come across many amazing and successful personalities, such as Abraham Lincoln, Thomas Edison, and George Washington, who became prosperous and legendary only because they had a very supportive mother. They all testified that their mothers were the only true motivators and inspirations for their success. Even those men who have done as much as they were capable of for the Kingdom of God, spoke glowingly and proudly about their mothers.

For instance, people like the great evangelist Billy Graham, in his book, "Just as I am," wrote the following words:

"In many Crusades over the years, I have devoted at least one message to the subject of the family. In my Depression- era growing-up year, I suppose we Grahams on our North Carolina dairy farm bore some resemblance to the fictional Walton family on television. It's easy to feel nostalgic about simpler times, but they obviously were not easier times. Nor were they necessarily happier times.... What we did have back then, was family solidarity.

We really cared about each other, and we liked to do things together. Jesus' word picture of a hen gathering her brood under her wings, fits my mother. She saw to it that we gathered frequently and regularly—and not just around the dinner table or in front of the radio for favorite broadcasts. She gathered us around herself and my father to listen to Bible stories, to join in family prayers, and to share a sense of the presence of God..."

On August 14, 1981, Morrow Graham quietly left this earth in her sleep and entered Heaven.

"*When word came,*" said Billy, "*I wept and yet rejoiced at the same time. Of all the people I have ever known, she had the greatest influence on me. I am sure one reason that the Lord has directed and safeguarded me, as well as Ruth and the children, through the years was the prayers of my mother and father.*"

I can relate so much to Billy. The unforgettable loving relationship he shared with his mother, whether in a secular or a spiritual manner, motherhood had the potential to shape his destiny and work towards enriching his life with unconditional love for Jesus Christ.

Recently, I read a story about a school girl who was disciplined by the school authority for violating the school's dress code. Then the girl went home and told her mother about what happened with her in school. This made her mother furious and she sued the school and the principal. Her legal argument was that neither the school nor the principal had the right to correct her daughter's dressing, as it is none of their business to tell her what to wear or what not to wear.

I have no idea about the end of the legal proceeding. The mother may have won over her legal argument, but she invariably lost on moral grounds because she didn't set herself up as an agent for the moral rectitude to her daughter.

Some people may argue: "*Why do we need morality in our lives, anyway; isn't it our right and personal liberty to do as we wish?*" My personal opinion would be: "*Yes, we do have the liberty, but the reason for morality goes beyond us.*"

A wise man in the sculptures put it this way: "*... so, enjoy yourself in your youth, young man, and be encouraged during your younger days. Live as you like, consistent with your worldview, but keep in mind that God will bring you to account for everything*" (Ecclesiastes 11:9 ISV). Just like that, my mother never forgot to teach me about the importance of morality in my life. She taught me, through her actions, that our ethics work as pioneers towards us becoming better human beings who will always be loved by Jesus Christ.

We can vividly understand that both Christian and non-Christian mothers wield an enormous influence on their children, teaching them every little basic thing that they need to know. Regardless of the religious differences, a mother will try her best to give her children the best of both worlds. However, Christian mothers understand that they have some work, assigned by Jesus Christ, to create a yearning for God in the hearts of their children. A kind of yearning that I have had within myself, since my mother gifted me my very first, precious Holy Bible. That day, I realized that my mother, regardless of the underprivileged life we were living, never forgot to encourage me towards finding peace and success. She made sure that Jesus Christ was the One and Only to look up to when faced with hardships. Just like my mother's way of thinking, every mother should understand that God should always remain as the centerpiece during the upbringing of their children. We just want to thank the Lord for a mother such as you:

"You were there throughout the years. Whatever we went through, and we just want to say that we love you so very much and we're praying that the Lord will shower you in love."

M.S. Lowndes

CHAPTER 8
Faith of my Mother

*"Father, I pray that Jones learns
how to be resilient. I know this
world is a hard place to live, and
while I pray that you protect him
from its evils and deliver him from
our poverty, I pray that you make
him resilient in all things."*

My Mother

My mother never behaved in a pessimistic manner in front of me. We were suffering from poverty at that time and she had no support from a husband. She could have placed the blame on bad luck, a cruel world, or even God, for leaving her to lead such a desperate life. It was her solemn right to complain to God about losing my father when I was only four, about where we were born (in Nigeria), about the struggles she faced as a widow and about our abject poverty. She could have whimpered about her fate of suffering from breast cancer as a widowed mother of six. BUT, she did not lose faith in God. She did what the best mothers do in difficult times, she persevered and prayed.

On a daily basis, she would lift her *"eyes unto the hills, from whence cometh my help"* (Psalm 121:1). Not a day passed by when she did not pray for her country, the widows and orphans, her children, herself. But, from what I distinctly remember, most of her prayers were for me. I can recall how much she prayed for me on a regular basis when I was a child. I could hear her vividly when she was praying; it wasn't that hard to hear something being said in a place which was barely-a-house anyway.

My mother was one of those many strong mothers who understood the divine purpose for motherhood and kept her faith in God for fulfilling her prayers.

> *"No man is poor who has a godly mother."*
>
> Abraham Lincoln

My mother's faith was very simple, but also very strong, unconditional and profound. Her faith brought heaven on earth to me when I stepped out of my domain of poverty. In chapter 1 of Luke, the story of Mary's faith of passing God the promise of a Messiah has been discussed in detail. Mary's faith in Jesus was so strong that she became the chosen one. Her response was astonishing when the angel told her that she would conceive a child by the Holy Ghost, who would become the Savior of the world. She said, *"May it be to me as you have said"* (v. 38).

It was Mary's faith which, literally, brought heaven to earth: when any mothers live by the faith in God, there is also a possibility of going through "heaven on earth." As a child, I was surrounded with poverty, shortage of food, deprived of a proper home and the love of father, but when I was home with my godly mother, I could experience my own little heaven on earth.

My mother's faith was divided into two prominent aspects. The very first was her belief in the word of God: she always believed in all the commandments and sayings of Jesus Christ. The second, she always believed in me, even at times when I didn't believe in myself.

It was my mother's way of assuring that I dreamed for a bright future by saying that it doesn't matter how hard life has been to us, I believe in you, and with the help of Jesus Christ you will become successful one day. If it wasn't for her prayers and faith in me, I wouldn't have been able to carry forward her faith and teach other children about it.

Mothers are blessed with motherhood as they have the privilege of bringing new life into the world and, with the help of God, the child grows into a much better human being. A godly child is born to a godly mother and a godly grandmother.

"For I am mindful of the sincere faith within you, which first dwelt in your grandmother Lois, and your mother Eunice, and I am sure that it is in you as well." 2 Timothy 1:5.

My mother put her perpetual faith in the power of prayer. She never turned away from Jesus Christ. She never renounced the church, no matter how difficult her life became. Through my mother's example and her unending loyalty to Anglicanism, my spiritual education began and my devotion to God emerged. As a child, however, I was a reluctant church-goer, preferring my bed to the pews, but my mother had a way to encourage and inspire me and eventually lead me to the path of God. Only a mother could have wielded such an enormous influence, and that is how she wrought my early spirituality.

During the times of hardship, my mother realized that her position in home, in church and in society at large had a lot of significance in the upbringing of her children, especially in the absence of a father-figure. Only an impoverished widow with six children to raise could understand the hardships involved. She strongly supported and empathized with other fatherless children and widows, and never forgot to pray for them when going to the church. As a single mother, my mother was my only role model during my childhood.

While going through single motherhood in a patriarchal society, the church played a huge role in strengthening the faith of my mother. I couldn't be more grateful to Jesus Christ for my godly mother who never stopped praying in the Anglican Church in our community. The church practiced old-fashioned Anglicanism where the tenet of faith included constant affirmation of our love towards our neighbors, and where widows and fatherless children were given special priority in the community. This encouraged my mother to pray as much as she could for the lost souls, poor mothers and their fatherless children.

My mother invested her time in the church as much as she could, because it helped her divert her attention away from the many problems of her life. Her mind used to rest when praying in church - the church was like a safe-zone for her. She thanked God for gifting her a place like Church where she could belong and learn more about her faith in God. In return, she showed her whole-hearted support for the local congregation, by sweeping and cleaning the dirt off the floors and yard of the church every Saturday evening.

My mother didn't know much about how to educate me scholastically and wasn't literate enough to teach me the basics, but what she did teach me was more vital than any of the educational institutes would ever be able to teach. She taught me about my religion and the wonders it does if a person keeps faith in Jesus Christ. Many others would fail to answer Jesus Christ and pray to Him when facing struggles, not my mother.

Usually, people abandon their faith when they think Jesus Christ is silent and is not or cannot help them in any possible way. Little do they know that these hardships and struggles only enter our lives when Jesus Christ want to test how focused we are towards our faith. Do you think it was easy for my mother to suffer from so much her entire life? Do you think it was easy for her to not lose faith in Jesus when she had to cater her six small children all by herself, with no food to silence their hungry calls, with no proper shelter to protect them from the outside elements? Do you think it wasn't hard for my mother to agonize over the pain of having a cancerous lump in her chest and then losing the vision of her left eye? Didn't she have more than enough on her plate to live with? She didn't lose faith in Jesus Christ when my father died, and she never had anyone one else to compensate for his loss.

She never stopped praying for much better lives for her children, even when she had no money to buy food from the market. She never stopped believing in me and loving me unconditionally, even when she couldn't provide us a proper shelter to rest in. She prayed daily and never resisted from going to the church, even when she found out that she has breast cancer. My mother, oh my godly mother! Even the accidental loss of part of her vision could not stop her from keeping faith in Jesus Christ, even after losing her left eye, she never stopped dreaming for me.

This passion for sticking to religion kept growing with the advancement of her age and she built it inside me by gifting me my very first Bible. She never lost hope in Jesus Christ.

Hope is a channel of grace that helps us continue in tribulation. When we lose hope as believers, we lose an essential part of what makes us the closest to Jesus Christ.

Remember Romans 15:13: *"May the God of hope fill you with all joy and peace in believing, so that by the power of the Holy Spirit you may abound in hope."*

When God's answer to your prayer has a future element in it, you need hope to make it from here to there, just like my mother had. If you're being tried through diverse means, don't lose sight of prayer and assume the church as an escape from reality.

"The prayer of faith shall save the sick" (James 5:15). Remember that Christ's stripes purchased your healing, and He still heals today.

Why are believers not praying today? Do we not turn to God as readily because we think our daily worries are either too insignificant or too unmanageable for Him to help us with? Or, most likely, maybe we think we've got it all figured out. But all these assumptions are wrong. God is God, in all circumstances, whether the problems are simple or endless, like not having food to eat as a child, my mother's being diagnosed with breast cancer and then losing her left eye. They are all within His prerogative, and He longs to hear from his children about everything in their lives—the good and the bad and the in-betweens.

One of the strongest attributes of my mother's, was her faith in God, which never faded with the passage of time. She formed this pleasant bond with the congregation and the church itself. Her love was unconditional and not just reserved for me or her other children: she loved the congregation, her hometown, her country and, foremost, Jesus Christ, with all her heart.

In return, she was showered with the love and blessings of the local congregation who never stopped appreciating her will- power and supported her in every possible way, even though they too were all living an impoverished lifestyle like my mother. With the constant love and support from the local congregation, mother's prayers increased. Eventually, prayer became my mother's invincible weapon to fight for the comfort of the souls of her children.

Just like a soldier protects his country by forming a solid line of defense, my mother's defense for me was through her prayers. I have seen many children who wandered away from the faith, or lost their true souls, only to find their way back because of the unceasing prayers of their faithful mothers.

I was never lost as a child, because my mother never left me alone. Even if she wasn't present physically, her love and prayers always guided me to follow the right path. A path from where I found for myself peace, self-satisfaction and love for Jesus Christ. Who else should take the credit for all of this beside my mother?

She was the one who taught me the sense of what I should be doing and the things to stay away from through her personal godly living. She couldn't read or write, but still managed to teach me about Christianity through her practice of godly living. Reading the Bible to herself or to me was out of question. Even then, she was striving to learn more about Jesus Christ and took help from the Church.

All that I have learned today about God, life, love and family, is based on the foundations laid down in me by my mother. I learned a lot from her in close proximity – a life completely dedicated to righteous living, truthfulness, faith and love for Jesus Christ and His people. No doubt, she will always remain the most major influence on my life and religious practices.

For me, Mother's Day is not confined to one day: every single day of mine is dedicated to my godly mother.

Mary, the mother of Jesus Christ, is the greatest of all mothers. Motherhood has always been a never-ending phase which is very sacred in terms of a noble vocation. But Mary raised the status of motherhood to even greater stature after becoming the Mother of God, the Mother who is "blessed among women" (Luke 1:42). Mary provides us with the richest and most inspirational picture of what the ideal mother should look like - my mother was wise enough to take her cues from the only one who excelled at motherhood like none other.

For Christian mothers like mine, the answer is simple: Motherhood is God's calling, like the way the angel Gabriel came to Mary and must be answered; a duty that ought to be carried out faithfully by every single mother on earth. Having a sincere faith in Jesus Christ doesn't imply perfection. All it asks for is reality with Jesus Christ. Such faith inhabited in my mother, it was at home in her, a comfortable place where anyone can reside. My mother's sincere faith transferred into me because she sincerely believed in Jesus Christ as our true Savior and Lord. She made me walk into the reality with Jesus Christ every single day, making me spend time with her in prayer and preaching Christianity. Before I made a personal decision to accept Christ, my mother allowed me to become a lay reader in our village's little Anglican church, this started as early as aged 10.

She made me confront myself with scripture and ask forgiveness from Jesus Christ. She taught me the power of love and forgiveness. My mother developed godly-mother qualities and attitude of submission, thankfulness, and joy in Jesus Christs, even when the Lord was testing her with so many problems at once. It did not take me much time to realize that my mother was not picture-perfect, but she did walk with God.

My mother handed down to me her sincere faith during her lifetime, because her faith was genuine and genuine faith is contagious. For instance, Timothy's faith could be marked from his grandmother to his mother. Timothy was able to see Jesus Christ in his grandmother and mother which, straightaway, attracted him to the One and only Lord.

But you cannot share something which you do not own. If it wasn't for my mother, I wouldn't be waking up early and going to the church by myself. If it wasn't for her, I wouldn't have shared my knowledge about Christianity with my friend and giving him the Bible that my mother gifted me. If it wasn't for her, I wouldn't have prospered in the future and developed a much stronger faith and belief in Jesus Christ. My mother made me see the evidence of her eternal love for God's words and commandments, and she helped me understand and believe that these were good.

God's Masterpiece

God's Masterpiece
God took the fragrance of a flower,
The majesty of a tree,
The gentleness of morning dew,
The calm of a quiet sea.

The beauty of the twilight hour,
The soul of a starry night,
The laughter of a rippling brook,
The grace of a bird in flight.

Then God fashioned from these things
A creation like no other,
And when his masterpiece was through
He called it simply - Mother

Herbert Farnham

CHAPTER 9

My Archievements

I would have been nowhere without the guidance of my mother. The sacrifices she made just to see me succeed, they can never be repaid, and they will never be forgotten. The role she played in getting us through our tumultuous times was heroic. The valor and conviction she showed, even when it seemed all hope was lost, was simply amazing. Our circumstances in the village would have easily disheartened even the bravest of individuals. Even with seemingly everything against us, my mother never gave up and pushed me towards my success.

My mother always encouraged me to study and to educate myself amidst all our troubles. Our village didn't even have a proper water system, but she never thought of it as a hindrance to my imminent success. She always thought of me as something special. She always believed in me and reiterated that I was meant for success and bigger things. How did she know that? Was it her divine motherly intuition? I will never know now, as she is in a much better place. I know this as a fact that she has found peace in the afterlife. A God-fearing, humble, and wonderfully fine lady deserves a peaceful existence, but our position was in no way 'serene.'

My mother, every now and then, used to explain that bad things happen to good people for a reason.

She was always a beam of hope for me. Every time she worked on the farm, it showed me what hard work really looked like. We used to work for hours on end in one of Modakeke's farm settlements. To my mother, it didn't seem like a big thing at all. As a result, we continued working up until the last minute of every tiresome day. Then the next day, we would repeat the same routine. This would go on for the majority of my childhood years, but she never made me feel hopeless in any way. She would work endlessly, so that I could get the necessary items for my physical and mental (educational) growth.

She always told me to concentrate on my studies and stay focused on the future. She always knew that this lifestyle we were faced with every day was not meant for me. My mother had made peace with her life, but she was not ready or willing to let me face her hurdles. She always took her time in making the right decisions, decisions that would prove to be beneficial for the both of us. I still regret being such a nuisance growing up - I was the average kid growing up, playing and running around with other kids, causing all kinds of mischief.

My godly mother never stopped me from playing; she never scolded me in a harsh manner to stop my uncouth behavior. She knew that as a kid, I was privileged to have fun, despite our 'unfavorable' conditions. She never stopped me from doing 'kid-things' due to her vast understanding. She was never that educated but her way of approaching life always had its elegance. These are things that cannot be taught, despite our level of academic understanding. The tact of handling situations can never be harnessed if it is not already present in the individual. My godly intelligent mother had this in-born trait.

She knew how to handle me, my father, my stepmother and my grandfather, according to each personality type. She would always find a way to coexist with them and make a better living together. This attitude made me appreciate her even more as she continued on her life's journey with vigor and optimism. For a woman to continue her life in impoverished West Africa with her small son, was a huge challenge. Especially, adding the fact that her husband was no longer there to support her. This was to be the challenge of all challenges with no apparent hope for success. My mother, however, didn't see this as a challenge but a responsibility given to her by God and Jesus Christ.

Seeing her conviction and solid point of view, made me a firm believer in Jesus Christ as well. I learned from her what an ideal godly existence should be like and I tried then, as I do today, to incorporate this into my life pattern. No matter how much of a believer I become, the amount of belief my mother had was unparalleled. She never lost faith at any (low) point in our lives. My mother could see the silver lining and God's purpose in every tragedy. She would often point out we were not different from other people, and everyone suffers from something at one point in their lives. This was our life and we had to live it, no matter what.

This optimism and belief are just some of the reasons, I miss her so much. She, with her approach, shaped me into what I am today. It was thanks to her perseverance and undying faith that we made it through the village's dark realities. My village was no stranger to diseases or ailments; many of the people from my village had suffered from cholera. We were both at the risk of getting infected and of the disease taking a heavy toll on us, but my mother was not going to let that happen in any circumstance. Whatever limited resources she had at her disposal, she used to protect me and herself from common ailments, such as malaria-: for this, she would buy mosquito repellant for night use to prevent mosquito bites.

Resources were the one thing we did not have in abundance, but my mother wasn't about to let that ruin our lives.

We made best with what we had and strived for a better standard of living. If you would consider any famous person, they normally have an inspiration which served them as a guiding light. My mother fulfilled that role in my life, and whatever she did or said will impact me for the rest of my life. The impact has always been a positive one, in which I got to learn new things, skills and situations. Many people do not realize that our mothers are the very first source of knowledge that we receive in our life. The mother shows us how to talk, react, and sit, among other minor and major actions. People should sit down and realize just how important a mother's role is in their lives. Only then, will they know the importance of the teacher, counselor and nourisher in our lives. They will know that they receive all these roles without even paying out a single penny. All the while, we spend millions on our higher education without giving it second thought.

We think of spending on higher education as a necessity, otherwise we won't be able to survive or be at our best in difficult situations. We spend our entire earnings in the hope of receiving tuition from the finest of institutions, as they have the best teachers and counselors. Now, imagine how much you owe to the saintly figure in your home: "the mother". You simply can't put the amount into numbers. It cannot be calculated, nor can it be proved statistically. It is something which we cannot contemplate, although it is given to us without even asking. This is the beauty of the relationship we have with a person who is commonly known to us as Mother. The teacher, the guide and the nourisher - all roles filled by one entity, without even a second thought. Do you get my point? This is what a mother's love is: it cannot be quantified, it cannot be explained, it is just omnipresent like the clouds, the sun and the moon.

This is the love which is not tied down by any limits, constraints or hesitation. It is a blessing which is given to us directly by God Himself. A mother's love is the trait which cannot be copied or expected from anyone else. No matter how strong a bond is with anyone else - a father, a sibling, a friend or a lover, etc. - it can never come close to the union between a mother and her child. This is because this relationship is based upon complete and utter selflessness. A mother never expects anything in return from her children, while "we," the children, expect a lot from her. How ignorant, cruel and selfish can a person be? Yet that's the way we are, and I am not putting myself out of this scenario. We only want food, belongings, clothes, toys and endless support from our mothers, and our mothers quietly cater to our needs, always. Wow! Simply wow! These are the thoughts which constantly come to my mind when I remember my mother. The cruel irony of the human psyche is that we only fully realize someone's importance when they are gone. During our glory days, such thoughts never come to our minds.

Only when the person's gone, do we realize that such a precious entity is lost to us. It is our curse, in my viewpoint, and I felt its effects severely when my mother passed away. All the aforementioned roles that a mother fulfills, she does so without any greed and selfish motives. She does everything on the spur of the moment and neither wants nor expects any compensation at all.

As an example, try giving your mother compensation for her services in your life. For one thing, like I mentioned earlier, there is no way of quantifying a mother's roles (as they have many). Even if you manage to quantify these and have the resources to pay her in full, I assure you, she will never EVER take it. She will shrug it off like it's no big deal and tell you to get ready for dinner.

This describes a mother in the purest sense: the teacher, the guide, the full-time carer, the comforter, the rock, and the one who nourishes you as well. What a person! Truly, she cannot be put into words and her actions cannot be copied.

The mother is truly the finest creation of God, and seeing my mother's journey through thick and thin, further reinforces my belief. My mother had served a dual purpose in my life: she was both the mother and father to me and she fulfilled these roles with exceptional merit.

She was overly qualified for it, as her guidance helped me greatly in facing life and all its inherent struggles. During my childhood, I used to feel blessed that I had such a godly mother, unlike my friends in the village. Their mothers probably didn't have the guiding nature like mine. Her attributes served as an example of God's Sacrifice, His love and His care, for me.

Activities common for the average child, like music lessons or any organized sports, were not part of my childhood because they were simply not available in our destitute, remote village. If they had been, without a second thought, my mother would have made sure that I had the opportunity to be involved. Still, even this didn't stop her from giving me fun-filled activities. We used to undertake in various physical and brainstorming activities, and because of this, I was able to boost up my confidence levels and develop my personality for the better.

I engaged in a lot of playful activities - I was not about to let my family's predicament halt my progress in life. Soccer had become my innate passion; even heavy rain couldn't stop me playing this sport. I used to play with children who were a lot older than me, as they were the only ones available. We also played many games, like swimming up the rivers that ran across the village. It was all a lot of fun, I feel gleeful each time I reminisce about my childhood. I used to line up traps for animals, and fish so that we could receive the necessary nutrition, despite our impoverished circumstances. These days were mixed with a lot of highs and lows, with lows making up the majority, but we adjusted according to the times.

My mother taught me to be a responsible person and showed me the way towards independence. I am indebted to her and her teachings, chief among these included cooking. She knew that if I was all alone, the least I needed do to survive was to cook my own food. She had incredible foresight, both as a trait and partly due to her experience in our destitute region. We needed to survive through all the difficulties, and cooking was a necessity: I needed to learn, and I did.

In addition to her foresight, my mother also had a respectful nature. She always used to treat people of all ages, with the utmost respect. We didn't have much for ourselves, but still my mother used to give a lot of respect to people who were in even worse shape than us. This was another trait that I followed dearly from my mother and this greatly elevated my respect for her.

My remarkable mother was endlessly generous with her selflessness and self-sacrifice, particularly where I was concerned. She always put me first. I recall many occasions when she deny herself, to benefit me.

I was born into a poor family, with all the troubles that come along. Though my mother mostly made ends meet, in order to put food on our table, sometimes, there still wasn't quite enough and she would go without food so that I could eat. We used to catch fish in a river close to our home, whenever she was free from working on the farm, and she would give the best parts of the fish to me, while she would only eat the meat on the scraps. She knew I needed the nutrition for my growth.

When I began my studies at university, my mother took extra work on other people's farm, in order to help pay for my school supplies. This new job covered only some of our costs, even though she always worked late into the night. She used to work by the light of a little candle, which didn't afford her much assistance and would tire her out completely, but she never complained and refused to stop, always wanting to earn the money for me.

I recollect studying for my final exams and my mother had taken some leave from her work in order to attend to me. She would wait for hours for me during my test under the scorching heat of the sun. As soon as I was finished, she would reach for her apron to give money to feed.

Upon the completion of my studies, I found a job in the city. It was my time to bear the burden and take on the responsibilities of taking care of her. She often hesitate to take whatever amount I sent to her because she believed that I wasn't stable yet, financially.

With my father's last breath, my mother had become a single parent. The responsibilities and struggles that came with being a single mother were tremendous. The majority of our neighbors advised her to remarry, in order to have help with all of the responsibilities, and for moral support. She knew very well the implications of a second marriage and how they would take their toll on me and, as a result, she didn't remarry, preferring to cope with everything alone to ensure that her dreams for my success were not hindered.

Even when she was diagnosed with breast cancer and became terribly ill with this and all and treatments and the surgery involved, my mother remained strong in her spirit, tolerating the utmost pain, and never allowed me to pity or worry about her, again, being more concerned about me, rather than herself.

She never let go of her dream for me, and didn't want her hunger, exhaustion, lack of money, or pain to get in the way of her dream being realized.

After all this time, because of my mother's prayers and God's will, I am a successful physical therapist with experience of twenty years. My mother had always envisioned me doing great things - that's what I am doing now - and I find immense joy in helping people. All my accomplishments are due to my mother's blessings and guidance, and I have no words to show the enormity of my appreciation and my gratitude towards her.

I now live in Calgary, Alberta, with my beautiful family. Thanks to my wife Tanya, who blessed us with our wonderful children, I am the happiest man on Earth, and this is all due to my mother's belief in me, and her immense sacrifices that shaped me during all those years. I would never have been able to continue with my life, without my mother's support - I only wish that I had done more for her.

CHAPTER 10
Never Ending Thanks

"That's who my mom is. She's a listener and a doer. She's a woman driven by compassion, by faith, by a fierce sense of justice and a heart full of love."

Chelsea Clinton

C an you truly imagine a world without mothers? I can't. I was hopeful for my mother that she would have a really long life when she beat the cancer. Just like any other child, who wants their parents to be alive and well, always; I had that prayer for my mother. However, as God had intended, my mother passed away through natural causes. Losing my mother has left a great void in my life.

I am happy, I am successful, I am healthy; but there is still a part of me that longs for my mother's presence. Her love, compassion, faith, and belief in me have forever been the sole driving force that kept me going through rain and shine. There were, and still are, times when giving up seemed to be the only option I had, but I have been extremely blessed to have my mother as my guiding light especially in the darkest hours. Even now that she is no longer alive, I find myself thinking of her and her way of life during our tough times, and I always find the light. It's like she is still here with me, looking out for me, making sure I am alright.

> "The moment a child is born, the mother is also born. She never existed before. The woman existed, but the mother, never. A mother is something absolutely new."
>
> Osho

They say the birth of a child gives birth to a mother. This is not just limited to the birth of the first child. A mother is born every time she gives birth. It's like a renewal of her vows of unconditional love, compassion, strength, and sacrifice. Every child is different, and nobody understands that better than the mother. I was my mother's youngest child and I was not an easy one to raise. I gave her a tough time throughout my "growing-up" phase, but that never deterred her in her mission – to raise me into a fine, respectable, and an accomplished man.

For her, the one true mission in life was to help us – her children – grow into decent human beings. And to accomplish that, my mother did everything in her power, and sometimes beyond. For her, success had just one meaning - raising her children into people who can go forth and make a difference in this world.

She never had the means to do all that herself. She worked endlessly. She struggled and strived day in and day out, through the rough times and the good (the good were rare in the beginning), and she never gave up. That is something I have learned from my mother, not giving up, even in the face of terrible adversity. You know, bringing up kids alone is no trivial task. You have to be there for your children in your own capacity and fill in the void created by the absence of the other parent.

After my father's death, my mother filled his shoes too. She was our mother, but also became the father-figure in our home. We didn't have much to begin with, but whatever little we did have, my mother made us feel that it was enough.

Writing this book has been an emotional roller coaster for me. It has brought back the bitter-sweet memories of my mother that will be an integral part of my life forever. While working on this book, I came across this wonderful excerpt from the screenplay of "*Big Stone Gap*" (2016).

> "*No one worries about you like your mother, and when she is gone, the world seems unsafe, things that happen unwieldy. You cannot turn to her anymore, and it changes your life forever. There is no one on earth who knew you from the day you were born; who knew why you cried, or when you'd had enough food; who knew exactly what to say when you were hurting; and who encouraged you to grow a good heart. When that layer goes, whatever is left of your childhood goes with her.*"

> – Adriana Trigiani

How true are these words? I am sure each one of you who have lost their mother to illnesses, accidents, or natural causes can relate to these words the way I did. No matter how mature you get, or what height of success you reach, the person you miss the most, is your mother. A loving mother is a blessing bigger than any other, and beyond. It's not just my mother who sets an example of great parenting and exemplary motherhood, you see mothers do that everywhere, every day.

They will sleep on an empty stomach, just to ensure their children have enough to eat. They will give you wings and let you fly, finding your own way without an inch of concern over whether you'll fly back to them or not, because they have faith in you. They know that the connection between you will always be there, even when you are far apart. They know that they have taught you well so that you will be ok, and you will always strive to do the right thing, and. They will see you soar high from the ground and still pray to God to make your wings strong against the wind. They will be there to heal you and help you and fly again if you ever fall down. And they will do all this without expecting anything in return. They wouldn't even expect reciprocated love in return – the love that they deserve and are truly entitled to.

"Our mothers always remain the strangest, craziest people we've ever met."

Marguerite Duras

I couldn't agree more. They are strong in times that can break down even the toughest of warriors, they cry when they are happy, they smile through pain, they are resilient through whatever life throws at them, they stand with us even when the whole world is standing in opposition – how much stranger can they get? Imagine if we never had mothers to do all that for us. In fact, try and picture a world without mothers. Can you? I know I can't. I can't possibly imagine a world without love, compassion, sacrifice, strength and resilience because, if it weren't for our loving mothers, I doubt we would have any of these stellar traits in us.

Our mothers raise us in a way that prepares us for the 'real world' but, at the same time, keeps us anchored to our roots – the good in us, the faith we have in God, and everything good in life that we learn from our mothers. For that alone, we need to thank our mothers.

The world today may see me as an established physical therapist with two decades-worth of experience and a successful practice in Calgary. But what they don't know is that Jones Onigbinde wouldn't have been the person you see him as, if it weren't for his mother. We were six siblings and I, the youngest, was only four-years-old when my father left this world. Some women shatter into pieces when they are faced with widowhood. Others, like my mother, embrace the situation like a challenge they must excel in.

I don't know what went through her mind and her heart when she became a widow. There must have been pain, uncertainty, grief, and fear of the future, following the funeral, haunting her at night,. The reality may have struck her hard, and there may have been times when she wasn't sure of how she would go about everything that lay ahead of her, but none of that came to us. We never found out what our mother was going through at that time. For us, she was always the epitome of unwavering faith and resilience.

She dealt with one challenge after another, making sure each one of her kids got a chance at the life she never had. We were drowned in poverty, yet my mother never let that bring us down. Even when she had nothing to give, she gave everything away in the form of generosity, kindness, affection, and acceptance. Even though we were poor, parsimony was not a virtue to her. She was both open-hearted and open-handed. She gave out of the paucity of our resources without hesitation. To her, giving was living. She believed that the genuineness of our humanity was wrapped up in the sacrifice and love we showed to others. And all this wasn't just limited to us, her children, but to anyone and everyone who came to her in search of help. That's another extremely significant life lesson I learned from my mother – to be kind to people and to help them out in every way I can. This made me grow into a humble, benevolent, and generous being. I owe it all to my mother.

The dreams she had, began with us and ended at us. If there were any dreams that she had prior to becoming a mother, we don't know about them because she never brought them up. Her life was more about us than it was about her. It's like that with all mothers – isn't it? Sometimes, I feel that life is a little unfair on these precious beings. They are blessed with motherhood that is an honor in its own right, but then, at the same time, their lives become more about their children than it is about them.

They change their routines, lifestyles, habits, and even align their dreams with those of their children. It's like they stop living their life, just so their children can live theirs. What changes ordinary women into phenomenal mothers is beyond me. Like Oprah Winfrey once said: "*Biology is the least of what makes someone a mother.*" In fact, being a man, I believe I can never get to the real depths of what it means to be a mother. I am just happy knowing that I was blessed with the best. However, like I mentioned earlier, motherhood is missional.

A mother is God's way of telling us that He is looking out for us. He has sent for us an angel-like mother who will love us, heal us, teach us, help us grow, and guide us to Him and His preferred way of life. It is His way of letting us know that no wrong is too big to be forgiven; that the sparkle in our mother's eyes when she listens to our dreams is an assurance that those dreams can come true; and that no matter where we are in the world, there will be someone always praying for us.

> "*God could not be everywhere, and, therefore, He made mothers.*"
>
> Rudyard Kipling

Nobody has a heart that can contain all that and more, except a mother. She will give up her dreams and take up yours just to see you conquer the world when you're ready for it. I don't know what dreams of her own my mother gave up for me and my siblings, but I do know that if it weren't for her, none of us would have been where we are today. And, for that, we are thankful.

I could go on writing pages worth of homage to my mother, but that wouldn't be an adequate celebration of my mother's loving memory. She was lively and cheerful, she was firm when she had to be (she was raising a boy like me, what else would you expect!), but she was also a friend, a confidant and a ray of hope for us all. This is one of the major reasons why, following my beloved mother's death on February 9, 2014, we had a Christian wake to celebrate her life. Yes, celebrate – because anything else wouldn't have been befitting to her legacy.

This is not to say that we did not grieve – we absolutely did, and we still do - but for a mother who fought through all the odds to provide a better life for her kids, grief wasn't the best way of saying goodbyes. During the wake, my siblings and I took the opportunity to reminisce about the life she had lived. We shed tears, but they were tears of joy as we relived the fond memories of moments each one of us had shared with our mother. Even in her death, she taught us to smile through our pain and grief – to hold on to the good things and be thankful for them.

My mother is not coming back, but the sacrifices she made and the enduring love she showered us with, left behind a legacy that will be passed on for generations in our families. Talking of sacrifice, I recall this beautiful quote by author Cammie McGovern (2010) in her book "*Neighborhood Watch.*" McGovern said, "*This is what we do, my mother's life said. We find ourselves in the sacrifices we make.*" That's how strong a mother's love is. It is a love that liberates us, a love that doesn't hesitate at making sacrifices, and a love that endures everything to give us the emotional, mental, and spiritual strength we need to make it through life. And then, there are the prayers. A mother's prayer, like Abraham

Lincoln said: "*I remember my mother's prayers and they have always followed me. They have clung to me all my life.*"

My mother has been my inspiration for as long as I have lived. It doesn't matter that she isn't around anymore, because she equipped me with everything I needed to make it in this world without her. Yet I feel incomplete. As I carry her legacy forward and as I aim to inspire other mothers with the story of my mother's life, I miss her. I miss that she is not around anymore, watching me accomplish all this. I miss that she is not around to see the difference that she still makes to our lives. I miss that she is not here with me, helping me with this mission I've undertaken.

However, there are two things that I am absolutely sure about. One, if the dead has the opportunity to look back, she would be happy and smiling from up there, knowing that I have succeeded in taking the path she always wanted me to walk. And two, her prayers still remain with me, like the shield that protects you from everything that may harm you.

No matter what I do, my infinite gratitude to my mother for every single thing – big or small - that she has done for me can never be expressed with words. For those of you out there who have your mothers with you, do you realize how lucky you are? Take the time to cherish her. Spend time with her. Tell her what she means to you. Tell her that your dreams lived because she let go of hers and that you know how much she has sacrificed to get you where you wanted to be – even when she never talked about it.

A mother is like no other. She is a shield, a mentor, a teacher, a role model, a pillar of faith, a support system, and a strength but, most of all, she is a mother who loves you no matter what and continues to love you even when she is not around. She is a treasure that cannot be replaced. She is the force that can fuel your success and the hug that takes away all your fears. She deserves your time, she deserves your love. Be grateful for the loving mother God blessed you with and make sure you make the most of the time you have with your darling mother.

I sincerely pray that all our mothers who are no longer with us find eternal peace in their final abode. And for those who are with us, I pray for them good health and a fulfilling active life. Amen.

Mother, I will be forever grateful for everything you've done for me. Although I apprised you time and again during your lifetime, that I love you, cherish you, and am blessed to have you, I want to say it again: I love you! I miss you. I thank God, day and night, for blessing me with a mother like you. And I thank you for everything you did for me. I am truly indebted.

Allow me to share with you a couple of poems that truly depict the nature and depth of a mother's prayers. See, how both these prayers ask nothing for the mother, but everything for her children. These are powerful prayers made with a pure heart wanting nothing but the best for her children. These prayers are a true depiction of the selflessness and generosity in a mother's kind heart.

A Mother's Prayer

Lord, give me strength just for today
To lead my children in your way;
Oh, give me wisdom, Lord, and grace
To show to them your precious face!
And help me, Lord, to teach them, too,
The things of Christ, so rich and true,
Just let them see in me, dear Lord,
Your holiness in life and word.
Keep me from sinning with my tongue,
From harsh, quick words that might have stung
Their tender hearts that trust me so
And watch to see which way I go.
Dear Father, keep my thoughts so pure
That they will always know for sure
My Lord has led me all the way, Lord, grant
my prayer just for today.

Anonymous

And then, there is this shorter one:

Help me, Lord, to be a good mother
And raise my children right.
Help me to make all ends meet when
money gets too tight.
It can often be a struggle to raise kids all alone,
Especially when there is no father in our home.
So Lord, since there's no father to fill
that vacant space,
Please make our home complete with love
And blessed with Your loving grace

Donna Winfrey